Raw Faith

The Journey

Into Trusting God

Brenda Murphy

No part of this publication may be reproduced, stored in a retrieval system or transmitted in any way by any means, electronic, mechanical, photocopy, recording or otherwise without the prior permission of the author except as provided by USA copyright law.

Scripture quotations marked (ESV) are from The Holy Bible, English Standard Version®, copyright © 2001 by Crossway Bibles, a publishing ministry of Good News Publishers. Used by permission. All rights reserved.

Scripture quotations marked (KJV) are taken from the Holy Bible, King James Version, Cambridge, 1769. Used by permission. All rights reserved.

Scripture quotations marked (NIV) are taken from the Holy Bible, New International Version®, NIV®. Copyright © 1973, 1978, 1984 by Biblica, Inc.™ Used by permission of Zondervan. All rights reserved worldwide. www.zondervan.com

Scripture quotations marked (NLT) are taken from the Holy Bible, New Living Translation, copyright © 1996. Used by permission of Tyndale House Publishers, Inc., Wheaton, Illinois 60189. All rights reserved.

This book is designed to provide accurate and authoritative information with regard to the subject matter covered. This information is given with the understanding that neither the author nor Radical Women is engaged in rendering legal, professional advice. Since the details of your situation are fact dependent, you should additionally seek the services of a competent professional.

The opinions expressed by the author are not necessarily those of Radical Women.

Copyright © 2017 Brenda Murphy
All rights reserved.
Published by Radical Women.
PO Box 782
Granbury, TX 76049

Cover design by Rick Schroeppel
www.bookcoverdesignbyrick.com

ISBN: 0-9983308-2-5
ISBN-13: 978-0-9983308-2-2

*To my darling husband
who has been my beloved covering and soul mate
for the past twenty-nine years.
To my sister Laurel
thank you for your continued prayers and steadfast faith
in me from the early beginnings of my ministry.
I value, appreciate, and thank you for countless hours
in prayer on my behalf.
To my sister Pearlie
there is none other like you.
Your special way of displaying your love
and affection to the world will never be forgotten or overlooked.
Thank you for your prayers, encouragement, and support.*

Table of Contents

~ACKNOWLEDGMENTS~ vi

~ What Are Dreams? ~...1

~ Why Not Me? ~..6

~ Personal Definition of Faith ~ 26

~ Raw Faith ~ 35

~ Now Faith ~ 68

~ The Substance That Faith Is Made Of ~ 73

~ The Evidence of Faith ~..83

~ The Value of Experiencing Faith ~..86

~The Feedom of Laying It All on the Alter~...........................92

~The Validity of Things Not Seen~ 98

~ The Expected End ~ 114

~ The Takeaway: What I Know Now for Sure ~....................153

About the Author..157

Now faith is the substance of things hoped for and the evidence of things not seen.

—Hebrews 11:1

~ACKNOWLEDGMENTS~

My deepest gratitude to my husband. During our beautiful years together, he's been—and continues to demonstrate, establish, validate, and prove himself to be—a man of integrity, dependability, patience, wisdom, strength, and many times, a voice of reason in my life.

Through his love, respect, integrity, and joy of the Lord, he has personally afforded me the opportunities to live my life out loud in such an amazing journey from both a private and public perspective. No matter what, he has always stood with me and only desires the very best for me and our household.

Through this book Raw Faith, I am able to express my most courageous moments of triumph, as well as my most vulnerable fears by trusting in God and allowing Him, alone, to direct and order my steps without judgment and doubt.

Thank you for being my best cheerleader, my biggest promoter, my coach, and my best friend. This book is a testament to our personal, private, and real journeys together.

I would also like to personally thank Vicki Mitchell and Zerlinda "Mona" Wilson for your labor of love in reading my manuscript in advance. Your encouragement and support before, during, and after the book has been a blessing to me.

~ *What Are Dreams?* ~

Nothing comes to a sleeper but a dream.
—Jake Little Sr.

During my childhood, my dad was always saying what I called proverbial expressions that, quite frankly, did not register with me as being something earth shattering, having much depth, or, when I was very young, really profound; however, as I matured, I quickly learned that a lot of the things that Dad used to say were, and are true, at least for me, today.

One of his favorite quotes was, "Nothing comes to a sleeper but a dream." Admittedly, growing up and hearing him talk like that sounded funny and witty at best; but honestly, as I live my life today, I have come to know that that very comment says a lot, and runs extremely deep.

In reality, I suppose what my daddy was saying was if one only talks about what they would like to do and day-dream about what they would like to one day become if the opportunities given to them, most likely, their dreams will never happen; or at the very least, they could be put on hold indefinitely. My dad realized that a dream left unattended would only result in what he described as being nothing more than just a pipe dream at best.

As a sleeper, the thoughts and images that one entertains in their sleep mode or state of being is usually a dream of mere images of an anticipation or desire that is hidden or rooted in the mind's eye that tends to forever elude one's true reality. At times, a dream may only serve as a sad reminder for most people of what could have been, or should have happened but never becomes their truth.

For others, it could mean having the right set of circumstances happen in their lives before they believe they are able to logically move forward with their ideal dream in mind. Still, some people are plagued and continuously worry about how they will make their dreams come true rather than seek God from beginning to end. From time to time, some may believe when they hit the lottery for millions, they would be able to make their dreams a reality, while others believe that for them, it will be when their "lucky" break happens and they are rolling in the dough, and then things will change for the better.

Dreams are pathways that can quite possibly lead to realities if one is willing to truly put in the work and complete their due diligence. Dreams are having the willing-ness to not waiver during tough times or when friends and family are few. Dreams are about setting out on a very real, tangible, and personal journey that can be at times, especially in the very early stages, completely foggy, confusing, and unclear. I call this the incubator laboratory period. This stage is early on, when no one can fully grasp or perceive the concept of what is being worked on or worked out, except the Dream Maker Himself.

Dreams can be exciting and liberating; they can often-times be met with life's disappointments, setbacks, and sometimes setups. They can leave us frustrated, bitter, challenged, and even envious of others who have seemingly made it appear easy in accomplishing their personal goals, at least from afar.

While dreams are definitely a part of life's journey, it is imperative to understand that as individuals traveling through our various walks in life, we have to become willing participants to see the dream through. We must learn how to become patient with ourselves and, most importantly, keeping an open mind with a thirst to learn and be taught by those who know a little more than we do, and have experienced a little more than we have to shed a little light along the way.

Whenever I encounter statements like "If someone would just give me a chance," "I could really do this and accomplish this goal," more often than not, I get the impression that this individual has not sat down and counted the costs, or considered the task fully through before coming to such conclusions.

Over time, as a dreamer without the willingness to put forth hard work and dedication to the assignment at hand and without a clear concept of what the overall vision is supposed to be could find themselves growing discombobulated or disinterested in seeing their overall dream come true as a result of focusing on the wrong things on the side-lines instead.

Becoming content with just sitting on the sidelines watching others' lives pass by while they are sprinting ahead to the finish line, this person could quite possibly watch their dreams dissipate one day at a time, oftentimes ending in a life filled with regret, sorrow, remorse, pity, and shame because they chose to not live in a state of readiness or being ready for change.

One of the noticeable problems I have realized with being content with remaining a dreamer is that it causes me to lie in a state of laziness, and sometimes, denial about how accomplishments are actually manifested. It doesn't necessarily start with stuff on the outside but, rather, by making a decision from the inside. Dreams are manifested by possessing the drive and the mind-set that all things are possible to them who believe.

For me, achieving some of my personal goals took a surmountable amount of prayer, perseverance, vision, dedication, resilience, and fortitude to bring forth what I was hoping for. Understanding the importance of the nature of the dream, the origin from which they were created, and the processes of what it would take to make them happen is another lesson in itself.

The importance of being able to recognize that a dream lies within us with a clear picture of knowing that we each possess the instinctive ability to bring life into something that was uniquely designed and fostered just for us is an incredible thing. Sure, others can duplicate what another has started, but only one can originate the true message that only God himself began in that particular individual. There simply are no duplicates of that dream had in store for that particular person.

In our world today, we see many examples of that all the time. For instance, the "new and improved" concept comes from an original business that began in 1902 versus an up-and-coming business that watched and duplicated the original business' blueprint and now calls the idea their own.

Dreams have a way of connecting us to that pivotal moment in our lives where we are somehow compelled to move forward in our endeavors even when it is at the risk of being misunderstood or not taken seriously by others.

Daily, I encounter people who you can just tell by sheer conversation with them that they are passionate about a particular conjuncture; however, in a short time, you can also watch them talk themselves right out of all possibilities by saying, "One day…"

Having a dream in our hearts allows room for more development and improvement to unfold. It means that we have not done it all; there is more to be discovered. Stay tuned—the best is yet to come. We must be careful that dreams are very rarely completed in one day or one moment. We must learn how to accept the fact that we have not completed it all nor finished it all in one simple setting.

No matter what age we are, what our pedigrees might display, what neighborhoods we are from, each of us has room to grow and it is up to us to challenge ourselves to finish what is started.

At the outset of any dream, I believe it is imperative that we ask ourselves some very poignant questions that can assist with getting the ball rolling, such as, What is the dream? How do you plan to move forward with the dream? Does the dream make sense to forge ahead now in your life? Lastly, does the dream have merit, and What are its dynamics?

Equally important is to note the pros and cons behind the thought process in the dream and the realities and purposes of how the dream serves its purpose and who it serves.

Is the dream pure in nature, beneficial to its cause? Does it uplift, motivate, and encourages others, and is it profitable?

I believe that every human being has been birthed into this wonderful world with a significant and unique purpose by the Almighty God. I believe that no one on this earth is insignificant regardless of how overlooked, underpaid, underappreciated, and sometimes how devalued others may be treated. In Christ Jesus, there is greatness in all. God created everyone with a plan and an incredible uniqueness like no other, and nothing and no one can ever change that aspect of your journey.

~ *Why Not Me?* ~

I am, more often than not, blown away by certain responses I get from others when great accomplishments are made. There seems to be a false sense of belief that gifts and callings are given only to a "special breed," or caliber, of people. Somehow it seems, at least depending upon who you are having this conversation with, there are those individuals who truly believe that their special gift belong to only a certain core group. How very disappointing it is to truly believe that lie.

Often, just by being involved in certain conversations or if you are simply listening to the views and viewpoints of others, you may find yourself hard-pressed to believe, based upon the conversation at the moment, that anything good or plausible can derive from another human being. For some, in their opinions alone, there appears to be a false sense of belief that God will and, can only bless, a certain level of people, nation of people, creed of people, and even a certain population of people.

However, Romans 12:6 makes it clear that God created all of creation with a talent or gift, and we are to use and take full advantage of it and use it all for His glory only! Every person deserves an opportunity to display their God-given ability for the betterment of kingdom building to God's discretion and pleasure.

In my humble opinion, in today's society, too much matter and concern is given to what others think, say, or respond to what God has fashioned each of us to do and to behold. While I think seeking Godly counsel definitely has its place on earth—and I do mean Godly counsel and wisdom, and not just sheer opinions and input of others—it cannot be the final word over your entire life. God should be included and involved from the very beginning unto the very end.

> *We have different gifts, according to the grace given to each of us; if your gift is prophesying, then prophesy in accordance with your faith…(Rom. 12:6)*

Armed with this belief and knowledge, we are all uniquely and wonderfully made and given a specific God-given and driven predestined plan by our Heavenly Father from the very beginning of time to accomplish much within the plan and scope of what He has predestined us to do. Under this plan, absolutely no one is exempt. Not one single person that has ever graced this planet was ever born without a true destiny and purpose.

Because God alone has created us and has fashioned us with such callings, equipped us with such greatness, ordained us with certain specifications, and set us aside for His use and purpose, we should seek Him relentlessly for the specific thing that brings Him, and Him alone, glory and joy. In other words, if I don't happen to sing, talk, laugh, or enjoy my life like someone else, others should not think that I am weird, strange, or indifferent, because I am not. I am just fashioned uniquely according to His purpose and plan for my life.

According to Jeremiah 29:11 (NIV), it is evident that His plan is clear for His people and it is intended solely for His purpose. Sadly, there are so many individuals who never live their lives for God and struggle daily trying their hardest to impress or influence others to simply " accept, approve, or validate" who they are and how they fit into this great God-given plan on earth. The truth of the matter is, stop trying, because people pleasing was actually never ever a part of God's plan in the first place. Romans 12:18 specifically states, "If it be possible, as much as lieth in you, live peaceably with all men." I don't think it meant forgetting about whose image and purpose you were originally created in to begin with.

"For I know the plans I have for you," declares the Lord, "plans to prosper you and not to harm you, plans to give you hope and a future." (Jer. 29:11)

Too often, too much time is spent and energy wasted on what others think about us. We crave, and sometimes chase after, what others may value or not value in us. Countless hours is spent in depression over whether or not we will be accepted or rejected, if we do not look the part, become the part, or can accept the part that others would like for us to play out in their "opinions" of us.

It is extremely heartbreaking and very deceitful to remotely think that even if we were to completely give our power away to others, they may only accept us if we are willing to totally erase all of our God-given identities for the mere fact of fitting in with a certain group, league, or gathering. Still, there will be those who feel they are superior to others because of a certain status quo or stand in the community. And our willingness to go alone just to fit in would only lead to even more heartbreak and disillusion. After all, validation doesn't get any higher than what God thinks of us, no matter whom or where it comes from.

In Galatians 1:10–14 (NIV) Matthew Henry Concise Commentary, the Cross-Reference Bible makes it clear

...in preaching the gospel, the apostle sought to bring persons to the

obedience, not of men but of God. But Paul would not attempt to alter the doctrine of Christ, either to gain their favor, or to avoid their fury. It is so important for us to not fear the frowns of men, nor seek their favor, by using words of men's opinion concerning the manner wherein he received the gospel; he had it by revelation from Heaven. He was not led to Christianity, as many are, merely by education.

Only God truly knows those specific plans that He has set into motion for each individual's life, and it is He alone who reveals those plans to us as we journey through this life and personal paths. Therefore, we must be careful about allowing others to plant various seeds of discord or confusion concerning our expected end, or what God's specific plan for us really is.

I had to learn never to ask someone with no vision to provide me with provision" for my daily steps in the Lord; Only God can truly order my personal steps in His Kingdom building for my life's journey.

—Brenda Murphy

Sadly, there was a time in my life when I didn't fully understand that concept for myself. I didn't realize that for every setback, it meant that God was setting me up for a comeback. However, had I only known that some of those setbacks were due to me not fully understanding and could have been avoided had I considered the source, or the lack thereof at the time. It wasn't until years later that I realized that during those growing pains I incurred unnecessary roughness, heartache, pains, and hurt all because I allowed others to inadvertently and temporarily attempt to make my life over into their plans and earthly designs, as opposed to living out what I believed that God had called and equipped me to do because I was a little apprehensive about going it alone, if necessary.

The strategic "comeback" came with maturity, learning, and experiencing God for myself. It would not come from a crowd, a person(s), a church, a pastor, teacher, leader, or otherwise. It came by way of having the willingness to be still and know (learn) for myself that He was, and is, the Lord over my entire life. He is, indeed, Lord overall and in all. Today, I know for myself these are not just mere words from a song but my personal reality, and for that, I am extremely grateful for these life lessons learned.

While being still may sound like weak or feeble excuses for moving forward, it was the very best thing that I could have ever experienced in my entire walk with Christ. Being still and being able to rest in Christ requires acknowledging that I needed Him more than anything or anyone else in my entire life.

The truth of the matter is, daily I gladly acknowledge and readily admit, "Father, I am nothing without you. I can do absolutely nothing without you. I wholeheartedly declare and decree that when I am in your presence, only then do I feel whole, complete, fearless, humble, and pre-sent. I recognize now that I only exist to do Your will."

I identify with the fact that daily it takes time, humble-ness, desire, willingness, hunger, and, more importantly, a discipline to become dependent and thirsty to seek after His perfect will for my life. I willingly choose to become weak so that the Almighty God would be strong in my life. What I realized the most in understanding that concept was that it became my daily mantra and that I had to literally learn how to refute my flesh, my fleshly thoughts and ways; give up complaining to a fault, whining; and stop stressing over things that were not remotely a part of my personal journey or the bigger picture for my life.

I had to rely on the fact that the Almighty God had a plan—in fact, He was the plan. He created the plan, and in due season, He would execute His plan for my life's journey. When I truly considered that the plan was created with me in mind and that God would use the plan for my life and His purpose, I began to relax and relinquish more and more of my will over into His expected plan for my personal purpose. And what do you know, life seemingly became much easier to enjoy because it was not about me but all for His glory!

As I continued to humble myself before God, I literally found that I was becoming more fortified, encouraged, and invigorated in His purpose. Daily I became strengthened and enlightened; and I grasped the fact that I was one hundred percent accepted as the beloved in His sight. I knew that as long as I was willing to abide under the shadows of the Most High, I could stand still and witness for myself the true salvation of the Lord.

No matter the trial, test, storm, situations, or circumstances, I fully embrace the fact that my God is more than enough to see me through, and that He is my God even when I am in what is considered to be a tight spot. Without having that understanding, I allowed my abilities and my talents to be pushed, tried, used, and sometimes even abused, beyond measure, especially when it was not necessarily appreciated or well received by others at the outset.

Not understanding that I was being taken for granted and often used as a display board for others to take the credit for my labor, just so it would be feasible for them, and then later attempted to discount me as if I, or my gift, didn't matter to the kingdom building at all was heart-breaking at best. Looking back at it now, when I see those individuals who hurt me the most, I give them a big smile and, if possible, a great big godly hug and say, "Thank you for making purpose happen in my life."

The truth of the matter is, without the pain, hurt, and sometimes intolerable treatment that I received from some folk, I probably never would have grown in certain areas or aspects of my life because I could have allowed my feelings, emotions, and perhaps my temporary circumstances to cause me to become too content where I was. You see, complacency will cause that type of knee-jerk reaction in one's life called stagnation. Stagnation, like still water, will cause things to simply decay even if it is the very substance that appears to be what housed it in the first place.

Without that unnecessary roughness, I probably would never have sought after the Word of God for my life as urgently as I did. I probably would have, spiritually speaking, during those painful days, just settled for mediocrity, pulling back from it all, not seeking the Lord for His guidance as I should have. Thinking that I may have missed my window of opportunity to be used by Him, giving too much authority over to listening to others' opinions, thoughts, and discussions over my life. I may have been inclined to believe that I had overlooked His instructions and will for my purpose and simply quit too soon.

However, one day, I concluded that surely through His death, burial, and resurrection on the cross at Calvary for my life, all of that could not have been in vain and that

He would reward me and shelter me from every storm and cause my latter days to become greater.

'The latter glory of this house shall be greater than the former, says the Lord of hosts. And in this place I will give peace, declares the Lord of hosts.' (Haggai 2:9)

Had I really understood my purpose and the importance of being properly nurtured and protected in the early stages of my journey, I am sure that it could have spared me a lot of unnecessary headache and temporary setbacks. Even to the point of avoiding some wolves in sheep's clothing; even though in today's time, some of the wolves appear to be dressing in more up-to-date fashions. Nevertheless, I quietly gathered up those stones and placed them in my proverbial satchel and used them appropriately at the appointed time to take me higher to the next spiritual level in Jesus's name.

After a while, I decided it becomes necessary and needful to simply retreat and take some much-needed time away from it all to rest, recoup, replenish, and become restored by the true Master himself in order to continue the journey and finish the course victoriously. I can say beyond a shadow of a doubt that the daily renewal of the mind during the journey thus far has been the greatest antidote for my healing process. What I know for sure is that absolutely no one can restore brokenness, tiredness, and heartache like our God can.

True and authentic deliverance comes when you get to know God for yourself. Coming into my own with Him for myself became real, authentic, genuine, and priceless. No veil, no curtain, no third party, no secondhand memo—just me and Him. I didn't have to receive my Word necessarily through what someone else told me or simply wanted me to know. It didn't come through what I overheard others say, but from what I know firsthand about what He is to me.

For me, it wasn't until I decided to get rid of the personal walls of separation between me and God, and daily come boldly to the throne possessing the willingness to share with him everything that concerned my everyday movement where I am able to truly be free in Him and confident in myself through Him.

The more I surrendered my all to the One who literally knows me, created me, and understand my going and my coming, I realized firsthand that with God, nothing in my journey would ever be wasted. Not one traumatic moment. Not one overlooked deed. Not one painful teardrop. Not one heartache over a lie someone spread about me, or a rumor someone conveniently started. I was learning that even in the midst of the density of the ashes in my life, I knew beyond a shadow of a doubt that God can, and He would give me beauty for my ashes, that even while being in some of my most horrid pain, when friends literally ran out of my life with a distorted report of me. During those moments, I was never confused about whom I served or what role He plays in my life.

What I did not always factor in at that moment was that God alone was bigger than my pain and greater than my most challenging disappointments, that the real purpose and work that was placed in me from the beginning of time was yet to begin, and that it was through my challenges and pain that true understanding of growth in God was being birthed.

When I learned that God would use the very things that seemed to break me and render me useless for the world's use, that they would become the very pieces used to rebuild my name, integrity, position, purpose, and plan for my life and cover it all under the Wings of an Almighty God, all of a sudden, the tears dried up, and I gained wisdom in knowing that this was not about me, but rather, it had everything to do with God and His ordained purpose for my life.

Failing to realize that, there were some instances that had caused me to temporarily lose my focus on what really mattered most. These things caused me to become inundated with unnecessary concerns about projects and things that really had nothing to do with my purpose at all. I mean, they were good things at the time, but not necessarily a godly purpose in my personal journey at all.

No matter how timid or afraid I may have been to be out front and used for the Master's plan, I knew, even from childhood, that He had favored me for a special purpose for my life. I accepted Christ as my Lord and Savior at the age of nine years old and I never desired to look back. The more I learned, the more I knew I needed to learn more and more about Him.

Of course, I lived in a real world like everyone else. I made mistakes like everyone else. I experienced challenges, concerns, complained about and experienced some of the same issues as the rest of the world; however, I never lost sight of God in my life. And thankfully, neither did He. No matter how lost or how far I may have appeared to be from the target, He always took the time to find me and bring me spiritually back home where I could be watched over and loved. Thank you, Jesus!

When it came to what I call public ministry, I was afraid of the criticism and critics that I knew would pounce on me like animals do when they discover fresh meat suddenly made available after a kill. Not everyone was vicious and vindictive, but for the most part, I did receive my part of the lion's share and then some. Even still, the call on my life was much more beneficial and important than the haters who anticipated my fall or me not completing the work at hand.

Public ministry requires a lot from you. It requires a sense of knowing exactly who you are in Christ. It requires an assurance that you understand your steps must be ordered by the Lord and you are merely a vessel being used and orchestrated for His purposes. You must not attempt to step into the arena of public ministry without the knowledge and humility of keeping your focus on what matters most to the Kingdom.

It doesn't matter how good you may be or think you are at your "craft" or "gift," you must never, ever go off on your own and forget about the true giver of the gift. Without Him and His anointing on your life, it is all worthless and short-lived. Someday when the applause of mankind becomes few, you will need Him to lead you on. When your charm, talent(s), abilities and degrees are no longer applicable to your earthly gifts, you will need Him.

The truth of the matter is, we can't sing professionally enough, preach the most prolific sermons enough, build a great house of praise and worship without the architect who first laid the true foundation being honored and adorned first. Without Him, absolutely nothing is possible, and the work will eventually, simply lie in ruins.

Even still, I desired the call, and I hungered for more of Him. I dreamed about the call; I longed to be in His presence day and night. There was nothing that I wanted more than to be a purpose driven for the Kingdom. I wasn't greedy about specifics, in terms of a position; I was just excited about the call.

I have always yearned, and still yearn to this day, to minister to people. When I see people, I see Godly potential. My soul rejoices when I minister to all people, any people—especially those who desire to know God in a real and tangible way. With a full understanding that ministry resided in me, I knew that as long as there was a world, I would never be devoid of opportunity to do so.

Being more conscious of my gift as an encourager excited me! I realize that stepping out into this realm would not always necessarily be met with smiles and pats on the back, nevertheless, the call on my life still drove me to always leave and escape my comfort zone to minister to others about the sheer goodness and faithfulness of God, no matter where, or what the outcome.

Every conceivable opportunity that I was granted to minister and pour hope into the life of another was like an out -of-body experience, right there on the spot. Even at the risk of being denied access to that individual's time, it was worth the risk during that specific moment. Having a chance to speak life into others or the risk of being rejected by others didn't matter because I knew that the love of Christ in me was bigger than anything I had ever experienced.

As I continued to grow in Christ and learn more of Him, one of my biggest challenges was the fear of being rejected and not being taken seriously by others. I knew beyond a shadow of a doubt that there would be those who would never accept my gift or the call that God had on my life, because they had already prejudged me and perhaps deemed me to be unworthy of their attention, or maybe because of my gender, they believed that I was ill-equipped to preach the gospel altogether.

Whenever I looked for excuses or an easier way out for using my unique gift, the more I felt the Lord helping me to discern that what He had equipped me to do, and the provisions in which He had allowed for me to operate in them, was good enough. Even in my nervousness, and constant feeling of being inadequate to carry out the command for that assignment, God still ordered my steps, and through Him, I was able to accomplish the goal set before me in record time.

The more others questioned my integrity, realness, and audacity to speak on His behalf, the more God steadied my path. And even under the spotlight of man's personal viewpoint of me, I was always assured that God was with me and guiding me through it all. Moments of quiet time spent alone in the presence of God changed my life forever.

For those times when I didn't feel close to His presence and I felt distant from Him, I knew that somehow, it was me that had temporarily stepped away, not Him.

Quietly, I pursued Him, and there He would show up in what I called my visions or dreams. It was in those poignant and personal moments of our time spent together that He never failed to challenge me or dare me to ever settle for mediocrity but, rather, dream bigger dreams, and for me to seek Him even more for precise details on how to give birth to every aspect of my life.

Today, it's interesting to me how many countless hours I spent questioning whether God indeed had a plan for my life. I mean, I read the chapters, I knew the verses by heart, but I did not always believe that it was possible for Him to use me, especially when I felt inadequate; however, I still craved to be used. The times when I felt unworthy did not cool my desire to be a servant of the Most High.

At times, because I was my greatest critic, and not realizing that because I judged myself so harshly from my own perspective of what a servant of the Most High should look like or walk like, there were days I could not be certain if God was looking through the same lenses as I was. I didn't know that I was leaving the door wide open for Satan to bring in misguided thoughts and motives from the outside to do the same through my doubtful and negative thinking, and render his claims of guilty against me.

Year after year, I literally heard, witnessed, or was told of others being affirmed, celebrated, promoted, or simply given a platform to announce their next level of achievement in the ministry. And by all intents and purposes, on some level, I thought that was my route to go as well in terms of being "ordained" by man. When the pendulum of that kind of opportunity did not necessarily swing my way, I asked, "Lord when is my turn to be next in line?"

Temporarily forgetting about what the Word of God had declared in Romans 8:30 (NIV). *"And those he predestined, he also called; those he called, he also justified; those he justified, he also glorified."*

Interestingly enough, as I studied this passage of scripture more, new revelation came to me about it. First, whom "He did predestinate, them he also called." To predestinate a person is to decide their destiny, fate, or determination beforehand. In other words, no mankind had any part in the matter at all. Not only that, these individuals would be foreordained by and divinely decreed and purposed by God only.

Not only is God the only one qualified to make such a call, He calls the call an effectual call, but one that is structured from self and earth to God, and Christ, and heaven, as our end; nowhere in this dialogue is there a slot for the opinions or help of mankind as to who they believe is suit able or not for the kingdom building, in whatever capacity God chooses to use.

Not only does the call exist by God, but the call calls us from sin and vanity to grace and holiness unto God alone. This call did not originate from man but, rather, from the gospel call. It's kept alive and vibrant by the love of God, ruling in the hearts of those who once were considered as enemies to Him to prove to the onlookers and naysayers that not only is this the doing of an Almighty God, but they have been called according to His purpose.

Not only is God the only One qualified to call, He is equally qualified to justify His ultimate decision making. None are justified but those that are effectually called. Those who stand out against the gospel call, abide under guilt and wrath. Whom He justified, them He also glorified. The power of corruption being broken in effectual calling, and the guilt of sin removed in justification, nothing can come between that soul and glory; this call encourages our faith and hope, and assures us that as for God, His way, His work is perfect in our lives, lacking nothing.

Not fully understanding that it had nothing to do with being "next in line" but, rather, everything to do with God's timing and his perfect will for my life. I now know all too well that man alone cannot bless or curse what God has called into existence by the signing of a piece of paper and assigning me an earthly position from their personal view point alone. After all, in my humble opinion, what man is allowed to build up, he is apt to tear down thereafter, so it's better to just wait upon the Lord!

Through painstaking demonstrations, trials, tribulations, heartache, disappointments, and unnecessary rejections, thankfully, I now know today is a different day. A different experience and a different reality as it relates to growing into my personal journey. My life is not meant to be spent as a twin to anyone else but myself.

Over time, through resting in the everlasting arms of Jesus, He has taught me, that the call for my life would not come by way of a checklist of rules that include do's and don'ts. If I conformed to the ways of the world, there would be a contest by which the contestants would have to jump through hoops in order to perform at the command of people at any moment of time during my spiritual walk. Neither would it be at the acceptance of people regardless of status or status quo.

My position in Christ would be solely at His perfect will and timing. Daily, I am coming into the knowledge that I was created in His image and exist today solely for His glory. Formed and shaped for His purpose. Used at His command. Kept for His explicit use and vindicated because of His namesake.

This predestination is to particular persons, who, therefore are called, justified, and glorified by God; it is the effect of God's divine grace in its entirety. It is the source of all the other blessings of grace, and therefore places us at the head of what others may think about the call on our lives, knowing this secures us from everyone else's opinions and doubts.

The Word of God continues by saying that whom He also called, even though some of us may have some or many afflictions during the call: there will be others who may be called to afflictions, and endure them while serving in the perfect will of God for their lives. Still, there will be some who are neither justified nor glorified; besides, the people of God, though they meet with many afflictions, between their call to eternal glory, their enjoyment of the call are not so much called to afflictions, but more so to patience under the call: their call is of grace, by special grace, to a peculiar blessings of grace, and to a kingdom and glory; and their calling is secured by predestination, and connected with glorification; and whom He called.

The Lord justifies and approves of the predestination who are sincere and faithful, on account of their faith and patience in sufferings, for such a person who may be viewed as one who is being plagued with various trials and tribulations one right after the other. God predestinates and calls. He makes them righteous by the imputation of the righteousness of his Son unto them; which is unto all, and upon all them that believe; by which they are justified before God, and the ability to escape captivity from the clutches of the enemy. He nurtured me and favored me for such a time as this.

Now, I can fully embrace and accept that it is in Him alone that I live, move, and have my being. Daily, I am fully aware that the Lord is the supplier, need-meeter, keeper, source, and resource of my every need, and with Him, I never have to worry about a thing.

The Lord is indeed my shepherd, and I shall not want or lack for nothing; He makes me rest in green flourishing, rich, plentiful and abundance pastures (emphasis mine.)

The Lord is my shepherd, I lack nothing. He makes me lie down in green pastures, he leads me beside quiet waters, He refreshes my soul. He guides me along the right paths for his name's sake. Even though I walk through the darkest valley, I will fear no evil, for you are with me; your rod and your staff, they comfort me. You prepare a table before me in the presence of my enemies. You anoint my head with oil; my cup overflows. Surely your goodness and love will follow me all the days of my life, and I will dwell in the house of the Lord forever." (Ps. 23:1–6 NIV)

Through embracing the Word of God, I know that my true worth and value cannot ever be summed up in the mere opinions and validations of any man and or woman. Thank God that I have lived long enough to know that my true identity is not based upon man's judgmental status of me. My true worth will never ever be reduced, resold, bar-gained for or with. It cannot be auctioned off, haggled over or debated. Jesus paid too much for me at Calvary for me to allow even my own emotions to dictate my true worth and value.

Even when I am struggling, He paid it all. When I am hurting and my body is being challenged to the max, He paid it all; and as long as I have breath in my body, I will open my mouth and declare and decree that I am still the whole and the healed of Him who died for me on Calvary and shed His blood for me.

I am so very thankful that I know for myself that I am free in Jesus, and that He that set me free is the same God that told me to go forth and in His Name; To believe and that I can receive when I call upon His Name; and that He will hear and answer my prayer, thank you.

Accepting the fact that every quirky, simple, unique, peculiar thing about me that was given to me at birth, God knew all about it, and He even designed it for my life. And at the end of the day, if He called it clean, if He called me whole and healed and delivered, and set me free and to be the head and not the tail, I dare say it matters not what everyone else identifies me as.

One of the reasons I now know why the challenge for me to get into the flow of the gifting that God created for me was the lightly dim examples that I previously painted for myself were too inadequate. It was through my imperfect view of my earthly window and lens that I was not able to fully grasp or comprehend the magnitude of God's greatness He had waiting for me to simply lay hold of.

At times, I compared myself to others who had a totally different heavenly design on their life than God had for me. I didn't know that the only race I needed to fully run was my own in the Kingdom of God. I had to discover that the journey for others would take them to different and diverse paths than my own journey, and that the strategies and designs that God would use to get another person to their destiny would be a totally different course for me.

Through time, testing, challenges, and sometimes trial and error, I was fortunate and very blessed to learn the les-son that it ain't over until God says it is over, and thankfully with God there were many, many do-overs if I was willing to listen and follow His instructions.

Over time, as I began to settle, humble and submit myself before the Almighty God and allow Him to direct, alter and change me in ways that brought glory to His Kingdom through my life, brought about immense and intense joy into my daily routine.

I was often so amazed with the unlimited, unspeakable, and immeasurable joy that I felt with the true acceptance of the fact that God knows what He has created me to be, and that I was perfect in His sight, lacking absolutely nothing. I am learning daily that I am already the righteousness of God, and that I can walk in my wholeness right now, resisting all sicknesses and diseases in Jesus's name. In fact, the more quiet and alone time that I spend in the presence of God, the more of himself He reveals to me.

And the more He reveals himself to me through his word, the

more I am able to release every fear, phobia, doubt, condescending emotion, and perhaps even the questionable lie that I have allowed he enemy, over time, to build a fortress around me, otherwise causing me to doubt my purpose sometimes in more ways than one.

The more time I spent in the presence of God, the more He showed and revealed himself to me in such ways I took for granted. For instance, whenever the Word of God spoke of "healing," I thought it meant physically being sick or in physical pain. I honestly did not understand or could not comprehend that while that is one aspect of healing; however, God also wanted to heal my mind, as well as my emotional state of being.

You see, I could not at times wrap my mind around God wanting to use me in His Kingdom building because my personal "perspective" and "view" of myself and what others thought of me was distorted and blurred at best. Attempting to not ruffle any unnecessary feathers, I com-plied with what others thought I should have done, rather than going with what I believed God for. Even though I could often carry out the work and was excited about doing so, I was never quite totally fulfilled because it was not quite what He had established for me to do.

God, being Lord over my life, continued to compel me to seek Him for more, and as a result, I immediately began to see change and to fully embrace and experience Godly peace within myself about relying upon Him for guidance and daily direction for my steps to be ordered. The notion to fit in went away. The ache I felt in the pit of my stomach when I was rejected by others, and at times felt a bit jaded, to say the least, began to cease and now, I was beginning to see more clearly.

Through the word of God, He taught me that I should never go to an amateur and inquire about what the Master knows for sure. The amateur's judgment, or skill set, is only as good as their limited imagination can take them, when I considered that none of mankind created themselves. Only the Master knows the real purpose and plan for our lives.

I continued to blossom and grow in the Word of God when I allowed myself to be made over in the acceptance of the beloved and Him only. I stopped comparing and trying to align my life, my gift, my call, my purpose, and my desires with those of anyone else on this planet. The only thing that mattered most to me was that my ways pleased God.

The more I aligned my thought life up with the life of God, the better I could more clearly understand His plans for my life. Embracing the fact that I was indeed the head and not the tail, above and not beneath. The whole and the complete of Him were so exhilarating for me. Understanding that until I knew and fully captured who I am, whose I am, and who truly holds my future, I would never fully be free to branch out and walk into my own.

So the next several years, I deliberately decided to sit at the feet of Jesus spiritually and not move until I learned from the inside out. I no longer worried or ached for those who, quite frankly, never looked for me. I could care less about being accepted by others. If I wasn't invited to some-one else's event and/or party, I learned how to enjoy my own party, even if it ended up being a party just for one. I learned how to entertain myself and thought I would rather entertain myself than to be detained by others who didn't care.

As the picture of my destiny became even clearer, I literally saw a difference on the inside of me. I became more fortified in my thinking. I realized that all those wasted years spent frustrated and "offended" was just that—a waste, because I really could not be offended unless I choose to be. It was then that I knew for the first time that I had grown tremendously.

It is an incredible feeling to know that I am in competition with absolutely no one except myself. I do not have to spend one more minute measuring, competing, aligning, or trying to fit with the mode of another human being. I spend my time now, evolving into the sculpture that God has already made me to be. I am growing and expanding at His command, and I will not go ahead of His plan for my life. My continual desire is to always run in my purpose.

As I continue to grow in Christ, I can rest in Him and take one minute at a time and not allow myself to become overly anxious about every little unknown detail about what happens next in and for my life. I can be genuinely happy about others' success because I know that we serve a great big God with unlimited vision and provision, and that each of his children get to move about the kingdom in their own "due season."

Letting go and allowing God to become Master and Lord over my entire being was one of the very best decisions I could ever make. Daily, I ask Him to please go before me, clearing my crooked path. Steady me as I go out into my day. Provide me with spiritual insight and in-depth wisdom so that I will not take the things that matter most to Him for granted or without gratitude.

Looking back over the specifics, when I entertain the question of why not me? I think to myself, I now realize that that question has no real merit because everything that God created has a purpose and God has every intention of using that plan in the lives of all of His children, great and small. It is up to each and every one of us to seek Him for our specific paths and not lose heart or focus on the way to greatness. If we choose to trust Him, He will get us there on time.

~ *Personal Definition of Faith* ~

Now faith is the substance of things hoped for,
the evidence of things
not seen.
—*Hebrews 11:1 (KJV)*

Growing up in church and listening to the pastor on Sunday mornings talk about faith was always exhilarating to me. I guess it's fair to say that I'd probably heard the word faith in church, like the average churchgoer many, many times. The only problem was, I really had no real concrete understanding of its true meaning for my life. To be frank, whenever I heard the word faith, I honestly thought it was for the elite and not what I called the "common" folk.

Sadly, during my younger years, the word faith sounded astronomical; out of reach for me. It echoed like thunder to a young girl being saved at just nine years of age. Being around others my age and listening to them try to explain their version of what faith was would always leave me puzzled, to say the least.

The young adults at my church would often refer to faith as being unreachable or for the "older generation" who had been a Christian for a very long time. From the gist of those conversations, I walked away believing that faith must have been for the more spiritual-minded individuals who outwardly displayed what my peers and I would call the spiritual lingo. In other words, those who knew all too well how to quote specific church catchphrases or who wore the churchy attire and knew all the church manner-isms, such as they were.

From time to time, I would encounter individuals who tried to convince me that their interpretation of faith was really being more spiritually minded and possessing certain outwardly material things than others. In other words, if one's appearance demonstrated at least in the public's view more materialistic things than their neighbor, then they were considered as one having great faith in God because of their possessions.

There were times I thought that faith was demonstrated through how words were eloquently displayed through prayer and who was chosen to lead it. In other words, if you knew all the names of Jesus and what they meant, somehow not only did it sound like you knew what you are talking about, but also results, were expected to happen. Becoming familiar with the scripture *"Now faith is the substance of things hoped for"* pretty much became something different to me every time a new episode or state of emergency happened in my life.

Because I lacked wisdom in this area, I thought if I worked hard enough, I could somehow convince God that if I believed and took His Word seriously enough, I could direct his goodness toward me in the manner that I desired. Because of this, I struggled needlessly. Thank God for His great mercy and unmerited grace.

As far back as I can remember, I have always wanted to be a servant used by God. I desired for Him to take me seriously, so I prayed in a manner that I thought was earnest and made all kinds of promises and decrees thinking that this was what true faith was all about. However, when things didn't happen for me in the order I believed that they should have, based upon my faulty understanding of how faith worked, I was very despondent and often disappointed when I did not receive what I had been hoping for.

On many occasions, when the pastor would say things like, *"Without faith, it is impossible to please God,"* those words alone sent chills down my spine. Without further in-depth understanding of that concept, I felt as though I was left to swim uncharted waters alone because I could not see how I would ever measure up to the standard.

While I am sure that I was not the only one of his congregants confused about what faith really meant, I pretended to fully understand its concept. Weekly I worried about making general mistakes. If I had a bad or immoral thought, I found myself questioning my walk and where I stood in my relationship with God.

Daily, without fail, I was constantly asking for forgiveness at the drop of a hat. If I even remotely thought that I had failed God in any manner, I tried in my might to be perfect and obey every command, law, creed, and doctrine (you know how long that lasted.) Having done all of those unnecessary, stressful regimens, still, at the end of the day, I was mentally and spiritually drained and was no deeper in my understanding of what the true meaning of faith was than when I first started out.

For example, if I ran short of money to meet my monthly debt obligations before payday or, heaven forbid, an emergency came up, I would say something like, "Now, Lord, your Word said…" I often used this phrase without realizing that I looked at the word faith only as a means of scripture that would somehow act as a thorough way to provide me the funds and favor that I needed to move forward and take care of my personal affairs in that moment.

Not realizing that faith was never designed or provided to me through a mustard seed so that I could simply wish, make, or conjure up enough strength to do it in my might. Faith is an instrument by which action is demonstrated in my thinking and then my believing and allowing God to bring it forth in His due season. It had nothing to do with my list of wishes, fears, and/or phobias.

Although I was extremely serious in the manner in which I used the scripture reference, shamefully, I must admit, it was for selfish reasons why I did so. I had always heard mainly through church, "Baby, just trust the Lord, and He will see you through." I didn't know much at the time about Psalms 37:4–6 that says,

Delight yourself in the LORD; And He will give you the desires of your heart. Commit your way to the LORD, Trust also in Him, and He will do it. He will bring forth your righteousness as the light and your judgment as the noonday.

I didn't have an understanding about what it truly meant to "delight" myself in the Lord. I was too busy fretting, worrying, stressing, and sometimes doubting in the moment to delight myself. I had prayed, set a time limit on when I thought that the blessing should show up, and heaven forbid, if the time frame given by the bill collector had passed, I was just waiting for the other shoe to simply fall in my life.

To delight oneself in the Lord is a privilege as well as a duty. It should be our honor to be able to rest daily in our Heavenly Father, and to be found joyously partaking of His benefits and His unlimited provisions toward us. We should not approach His throne as though He has somehow let us down and now we have to remind Him of our disappointments or the fact that we may think that He is slow in delivering our blessings on time.

I am reminded in Psalms 37 that God has promised to gratify not the appetites of the body, and the ungrateful wishes of our human flesh or fancies, but the desires of the renewed, sanctified soul. So perhaps the question we should ask ourselves is this: what is the desire of the heart of a good man or woman? Is it to simply grab and go from God? Is it to inquire of Him to provide for us whatever we think, or even believe, we deserve to have?

Our true delight should reflect that it is an honor to know, love, serve, and respect an awesome God. It should be our desire to commit our way unto the Lord of all and over all; the very first thing we should do in the morning when our eyes open and before getting out of our comfort-able beds, is accept the blessings filled with grace and mercies that He has allowed to cross our path.

It should become habitual for those of us who make Him Lord over our lives to simply and eagerly cast our burdens upon the Lord, the burdens of our care. We must roll it off ourselves, not allow ourselves to become afflicted and perplexed with thoughts about future events, but refer them to God alone.

We must become disciplined not to run immediately to other flesh-and-blood beings that do not have the answers for our breakthroughs, trials, and our situations. We must be extra careful not to roll our stones of issues and circumstances onto the backs and shoulders of others, who may not be 100 percent sure of how their own temporary trials will work out.

We have to learn that by prayer, supplication, and total dependence upon the Almighty, Sustained, Capable, and Exceedingly Worthy God, we can present our circumstances and all our cares before the Lord, and trust in Him to bring us through every trial, every time. When we learn how to rely, rest, and depend upon the Lord and leave the situation with Him, the promise from Him is very sweet: He shall bring that which we hope for to pass, whatever it is, which thou has committed to Him.

Although I was asking sincerely, deep down, I wasn't utterly convinced as to whether or not God would truly answer me, because somewhere along the line, I was including myself in the equation instead of relying solely upon the Lord for His help alone; because He loved me and cared for me whether I prayed or not. Had I only known that being able to rely on, trust, and rest in God would be an added bonus, I would have made that decision sooner rather than later, if only I knew better at that time.

Many days I spent wondering why the greater things that I

believed God had for me were near, but somehow they always seemed to elude me when I searched for them the most. Believing that there was so much more for me than what I had temporary access to, I decided to dig deeper and seek out the answers in sincerity for myself.

While in search of more profound meaningful answers for myself, I came to the conclusion that faith was far more reaching than a lucky break or a chance happening. I learned that faith is a belief that complemented my daily hope. In fact, faith complemented my hope in God. It would serve as an introduction to my best that was yet to come.

I learned by walking it out, that when my faith + my hope + my belief come together, it would set the tone for my greater expectations. An example would be this: when-ever I pray to God for a specific thing, like more peace in my personal life, I would go to the Word of God and find out what the Word has to say about peace. I didn't just stop at one scripture reading. In my research, I considered several. Over time, I found at least five specifics to encourage me along the way:

"When a man's ways please the LORD, He makes even his enemies to be at peace with him." (Prov. 16:7)

"You will keep him in perfect peace, whose mind is stayed on You, because he trusts in You." (Isa. 26:3)

"Peace I leave with you, My peace I give to you; not as the world gives do I give to you. Let not your heart be troubled, neither let it be afraid." (John 14:27)

"These things I have spoken to you, that in Me you may have peace. In the world you will have tribulation; but be of good cheer, I have overcome the world." (John 16:33)

"Be anxious for nothing, but in everything by prayer and supplication, with thanksgiving, let your requests be made known to God; and the peace of God, which surpasses all our understanding." (Phil. 4:6–7)

Isaiah 26:3 (KJV) says, *"Thou wilt keep him in perfect peace, whose mind is stayed on thee: because he trusteth in thee."*

I realized that God has not only provided me with the answer to my prayer, He has also laid out the process for me to receive my desired prayer request. There it was, laid out for me. Being able to trust in God alone provided me the peace and harmony that I needed to move forward. I realized after reading this verse over and over again that it would not do me any good to continue reading the words, unless I was willing to rest or trust that He alone could keep me in what I was asking for.

Through time, I was able to comprehend in that moment that trusting in God afforded me the opportunity to rest and to be assured that I can rely upon God's ability to keep me and to safeguard me no matter what came against me. However, I needed to take the Word of God as a gift and receive His offering by choosing not to fret and become anxious about anything.

In that instance, I learned that faith is the set deposit accompanied by expressed assurance that God is more than able to do exceedingly above all that I can ask or imagine, not by my limited abilities or efforts, but because God is well able to do so when I look to Him for guidance.

As I continue to grow in Christ, I am realizing that faith is having the humbleness and the perseverance to wait out the expectation until the due season for me has arrived. When is the due season, you might ask? Well, when it's due or it's ready to be revealed by God. Faith, to me, is setting my mind, which I call the heart of the matter, in direct alliance with the will of God for my life and being unwilling to compromise otherwise.

Faith, for me, is coming directly into agreement with God about my situation and releasing my hands and mind set totally from the matter. While this is not necessarily the easiest thing to do, it is a plausible and conceivable concept. Faith is trusting in the Almighty with what I am not able to see around the corner for my life, or my future.

Faith is my standing still and knowing that He alone is my Redeemer, my Healer, and the Keeper of my soul and my circumstances; it is unequivocally standing on the truth that the Lord is my "shall not want for nothing" God. I can personally attest to what it means to operate in pure faith, being able to soar at quantum leaps at times in what seemed to be effortlessly without boundaries during specific situations.

In my years of personal relationship with God, I now view faith as a muscle that must be worked daily. Faith for me acts as a builder or a prerequisite to build upon for that "expected end." In other words, if I don't expect anything to happen good in my life, I can pretty much expect nothing good to be gained from it.

Faith sets the tone for what I am hoping and trusting God for. In other words, I don't just want the matter in my life to work out from a one-sided perspective (mine). I want my heart's desire (my true kingdom passion) to work out for my total good; and only God can provide me with that guarantee and assurance.

Through faith, I know beyond a shadow of a doubt that I now have access to a hope that is non-fleeting or non-perishing. It's guaranteed not to fail me in the time of trouble or adversity. It's everlasting and everlasting and everlasting because it came from the Word of God himself. Hope is a bridge in which I am safe to travel and venture across to the other side without wavering to victory.

In fact, faith is being on the other side of victory beckoning me to cross over safely to the other side in the name of Jesus. I know that to be a fact in my life because now I realize that He just didn't deliver me— He brought me out of it (meaning He carried me out, transferred me out, and delivered me out) and placed some distance between me and the issue at hand.

Faith is not my last resort—it is my first and only stead-fast option. It's my dependable, reliable, ground-breaking resounding response to everything happening in my life. Faith is my get-out-of-jail card when the enemy is trying to get me to fold when I am under worldly, ungodly pressure.

My faith is the necessity on which my confidence and earthly trust is based upon. Not my will Lord, but thine and thine only be done in every situation of my life. Daily, my hope in the Word of God provides me with a plethora of benefits. Benefits like my peace, my hope, my joy, my wisdom, and my healing, just to name a few.

~ Raw Faith ~

The *Merriam-Webster Dictionary* describes the word *raw* as

"Being in or nearly in the natural state; not processed or purified likened to raw fibers; not diluted or blended, unprepared or imperfectly prepared for use, not being polished, finished or processed form, not having the surface abraded or chafed, very imitated."

In my earlier years of employment, I recall working as a call center customer service manager. I had become well acquainted with stress and tight deadlines, the pressures of meeting this goal and that goal, challenges and expectations. While I rose to the occasion weekly and monthly, my heart was becoming more and more removed from the unfilled moments of winning and temporary celebrations of meeting month-end quality goals for my work.

One day, one of my employees came to me and said, "I have observed ever since you returned from your last conference, you have not been the same. I mean you still smile, you are attentive to your team's needs, but you seem to be somewhat preoccupied by something else. Are you okay? Is there something that you want to share? I know you are my supervisor, but you always take the time to listen to us, so I thought I might ask you if you needed anything?"

Right then and there, what that employee did not know was that his words grabbed my heart and caused me to shift in my complacency and thinking. It caused me to question why I was struggling to move in the direction to which I felt, for some time that God was leading me but I was just too afraid to move.

My thought was how in the world was this young man able to see my heart and my heart's desire from what I thought was hidden from the public's view and discernment? Could he have known that I had privately been praying for God to give me a sign and direction of what my next move should be and when it should happen?

In November 2003, while on sabbatical from my job, God defined for me a very specific ministry, and He even gave me the name for it. It would be birthed as Innovative Ministries , Inc., A Season of Change. He said that my minis-try would be one that emulates a courtesy truck that comes along to help individuals who may need roadside assistance from time to time, provided by Him, through my guidance, direction, and compassion along the way.

You see, Innovative Ministries is not about changing people to conform to my religious beliefs or concept, for I have none that matter, but rather, it is to serve as an enabler to encourage, motivate, and lift up my brothers and sisters who just simply need prayer, guidance, strength, and love without judgment to keep moving forward in their lives, realizing that God will and can do the rest.

I enjoy every aspect of ministry. The challenges, the pull, the drive, the thriving of it all. I especially love the call, and understanding the purpose of it all, makes it even more special. Every time a conference was completed, I was drawn more and more into its aftermath. I found myself longing to do more for the kingdom at every level imaginable.

However, while I wanted to go into ministry full-time, I couldn't see or understand how I was to do so without an income to help support my household needs, let alone continue the ministry, as it should be. I could not see at the time how I was to possibly shift into what I wanted to do verses what was necessary to do to stay afloat. While my covering (Audie) was extremely supportive of me and the ministry, I knew that we lived in a real world with real monthly responsibilities. So I meditated on this scripture for support:

> *In thee, O LORD, do I put my trust; let me never be ashamed: deliver me in thy righteousness. Bow down thine ear to me; deliver me speedily: be thou my strong rock, for an house of defense to save me. For thou art my rock and my fortress; therefore for thy name's sake lead me, and guide me.* (Ps. 31:1–3)

Each day became a real struggle for me to go to work. It wasn't that I didn't necessarily enjoy my job, but my heart was no longer there. I continued to work there for eight years, and I know without question that I gave everything I had and with everything that was assigned to me to do, I endeavored to complete it. I enjoyed working with my various teams and coworkers.

I enjoyed making a difference in any manner that I could. But still, at the end of the day, it was obvious that the company and I were moving in two different directions. The company was changing; and quite frankly, so was I.

Daily I endured belligerent and screaming customers and managers who skipped out on their share of the workload; the constant mishandling of how some managers and teams were treated versus others who seemingly skated by time and time again and were openly rewarded for work undone.

After a while, this began to wear on me, and I earnestly began seeking God for something greater at this point in my spiritual walk. It didn't matter the cost—I merely wanted out. I desired the greater things God had for me even though I didn't know what exactly that was. I was more than willing to search for them into the deep.

Little did I know that this search would send me on what I called a world wind quest into some very rough terrain, perhaps deeper than I imagined and far reaching that I expected. Still, I knew once the search began for me, there would be no turning back or around, I was thirsty and desired more.

The meaning of raw faith began honestly on my quest for a deeper relationship with God. I now know that in order to move forward into the deep, the testing will come sometimes from various directions and individuals; but moving forward is, and was, my only option. Needless to say, along the way, I thought I was secure in sharing my heart with some people who regularly smiled in my face, who ate meals at our home and occasionally spent the night. Boy, was I ever wrong. Was I ever deceived!

Now, ironically, some of those very people who I once opened my heart, home, and hope to not only stabbed me in the back, but whenever our paths crossed, some of them acted as though they didn't even know my name. In reality, they sold me out the moment that time provided convenience and profitability for them.

All the while, they were being sent out to scout out my intentions. Tried as they might, they even went so far as to attempt to blow out the light that God had placed in me. I know now that the thief or thieves came not only to steal and to kill what God had already established deep down in my being, they were also very desperate they even decided to lay in wait in an attempt to hold me up, in an effort to at least delay my destiny and my arrival at the appointed place that God had already established for me to enter into. But God…

There were days while I was seeking the face of God for His complete direction for my journey into the ministry that required most or all of my immediate attention to details. It would be during those trying moments that I could have used the prayers and the support of true believers in my life; needless to say, there were none from outside my immediate home camp. I refused to give in to the pressures and the persuasions of the outside forces that wanted nothing more than to see me fail, falter, and, at best, finish last—or, at the very least, simply get into a fetal position and declare defeat over my own life and God's plan for me…even still, but God!

Even when daunting tasks seemingly were ever present before me, I chose to move forward, determining each and every step of the way that my greater was just one step ahead of me, and that by continuing to keep my eyes on the prize, I knew the latter would be so worth every effort with every Godly, deliberate step I would take.

Spiritual doors that were previously flung wide open for me to enter into for speaking engagements were now visibly shut with the padlock left hanging on the outside for all to see and whisper about. Some of those doors readily displayed a proverbial sign that read, "Not wanted anymore. Not appreciated anymore." And some just didn't know what to write, so they left the slate blank (Jesus)! However, thanks be to God, despite the deliberate roadblocks laid out for me, I still had one more "nevertheless" left in my personal praise and worship.

By now, I was coming to the conclusion that what didn't kill me, deter me, caused me to jump overboard, caused me to lose my Godly mind, or run and hide was forcing me into becoming something greater than I could dream, think, or even imagine for myself. The more people walked out of my life, the more God showed me: *Brenda, I am making room for you, baby girl. Less really is better. Don't worry. By and by, you will see it for yourself…*

All praise and glory goes to my Lord and Savior! Funny how God had used my voice to minister in various aspects in churches and events for His good; and in that moment, the people who were previously open and receptive to hearing God speak through me, now found themselves struggling to remember my name or the benefit I had previously provided to them and their ministry.

However, as my godly gift was making room for me to advance, the enemy was becoming increasingly angry and very upset and wanted nothing more than to replace and displace me for good. Not being very astute at that time in the gift of prophecy, or what I called a word of exhortation, God still sent someone to me each time and provided me a way of escape beyond my comprehension.

There were times when I was attacked viciously by some who proclaimed to love me by day but despised my gift and my name by night. God still held a hedge around me and my family, and I was able to move forward and beyond the boundaries and the corridors of mankind's evil intentions. There were other times that I taught class, preached a sermon, gave words of healing and exhortation to others standing wounded myself before certain congregation members, wounded, injured, and broken by some of the very people that called me friend to my face. These people attempted to insult my intelligence, despise my gift, and pretended to be my friend. These were people I tried to help, and at times, I am sure that I did, who joined in with others to scandalize my name.

I really believed that some did not think that I had the ability or the sense to know that they were not for me, or simply just tolerated me because they may have thought that I could not do any better, but I want to say today that even then, there were things and situations that were always revealed to me, but my intentions attempts were to love them despite how they felt about me.

Although being persecuted, looked over, and uninvited to the tea and crumpets fellowship, in time and by and by, I learned how to have my own parties. I learned, how to celebrate the fact that Jesus, and Him alone died for me. He was the one that sheltered me and kept me from my early existence until now. While I don't want to start any rumors, but I sure enough believe that He will be the one who will continue to keep me until the end.

There were days in my raw faith venture that I didn't even want to be bothered with the public's view because my name had been mishandled and scrutinized by malicious, evil, conniving backbiters. I believe that my name had been sold out to anyone who would listen to the negative talk. Isn't that how some things are? People in the world today would much rather listen to your hardships rather than join in with you in your true worship. They will have the nerve and the audacity to say sometimes, out loud, when you praise Him too much, "Does it really take all of that?" There were some individuals who didn't have any previous knowledge of who I was yet; they questioned my very purpose of being in the ministry. They hated me without a cause, sometimes even before the last wound properly healed.

Yet and still, I was thirsty for more of God and His pro-visions for my life. So without excuse, I went after what I loved the most—His Name and what soothed and calmed all of my fears and doubts, His grace and mercy. I would often steal away and say to God, "Lord, I will go just as long as you go before me and make all of my crooked ways plain. I am willing to go."

I continued to seek God for direction and understanding about why some of the yearly events I was previously privileged to attend were now struggling to come up with last-minute excuses as to why they were not able to contact me due to them "misplacing" my phone number or "not knowing" if I would be interested in taking on the assignment, so according to them, they didn't bother to contact me at all. The interesting thing about that was previously, over the last four to five years, it never hindered them before.

Not only that, but I noticed that suddenly, the usual calls were becoming fewer and fewer, until finally there were none. When I would see some of the ministry leaders and pastors out and about, they almost at times would walk by me and not even speak, unless I spoke first. Some made futile promises to call and invite me out to their annual women services or various programs; however, the call(s) never materialized.

Over the next several years, the verbal and or personal invitations altogether stopped coming in. It was sheer silence for at least three years where speaking engagements were concerned. I ached inside and felt so abandoned by the leaders of God's people, the church, and at times by God Himself. The pain was most unbearable when I knew in my heart of hearts that I only came to serve, not to harm or do anyone a disservice. In the end, I realized none of that mattered to my enemies because being in the group or the clique was more important than the truth or the facts for most of them.

I was being deliberately ostracized all because I loved Jesus and it showed. There were people who literally believed that I was out to try to take over certain aspects of the church and what they deemed as their place on certain pews and sections of the church. Even still, there were some who gathered in groups to plot my spiritual demise at any cost, and run back like worldly spies to provide their non-spiritual side of their findings.

Not one person semi-close to me ever took the time out to personally ask me my intentions, plans, goals, or desires. They simply took their own conjured-up thoughts and ran with it, never once stopping to find out the truth of it all. When I tried to fit in and associate myself with some of them over the years, I was shunned and treated like an out-cast, without a purpose or plan. It became evident that the lines were being drawn. Go or stay. Because I was no longer welcomed in the sister-sister cupcake circle.

Knowing that it was not my plan to ever deceive, hurt, or make a play to take over anything that didn't ordinarily belong to me, I still tried to remain faithful, diligent, and hopeful to positions that I held and work diligently to make a difference. It seemed that the more I tried, the more blatant it became that I was not approved of or wanted for that matter. I felt like an outcast. In disbelief, I spent weeks, and even months, trying to figure out what I had or was doing wrong. I refused to believe that I was being hated because of God's purpose for my life.

I literally could not understand, for the life of me, why people would be upset about the call God has on my life. I mean, didn't everyone have a call, or at least a cause to serve God? Why were people so angry and upset, misguided and jilted because of one woman who simply wanted more from God and wasn't afraid to go after it and more importantly, who knew that God loved her and wanted her to continue to grow.

After being in pain for months, I was still required to teach and minister, regardless of my personal pain and anguish. It didn't matter to others how they treated me and talked behind my back; and sometimes depending on who they were, they often attempted to throw subtle hints in my face. These people who were intent on spreading ungodly rumors and lies did so without any real knowledge or wisdom about me at all. They didn't care about the pain they were personally inflicting upon me. Their private agendas were all that mattered at the time.

There were times I would hear my ministry being talked about in public places by specific people in a joking manner. Comments like "You don't have to wear your skirts or dresses down to the floor to be saved." "Does it take all that to serve the Lord." "So you think that you are Ms. Holy Roller?"

And some of the church members would break out in a haughty laugh at my expense, of course. I honestly thought that I had temporarily landed on another planet because I could not grasp their cruelness or intentional daggers.

Daily, I would ask God, Why the pain? Where had I gone wrong, even going so far as to ask Him to please remove me from it all. I was never going to deny Him or my personal call, but I was willing to walk away from what-ever the church members thought that I was trying to steal, borrow, rent, or lease from the church or its name. Being a "member" never excited me; being a part of the body of Christ was where my personal joy resided.

I agreed to serving God with my whole heart, not to being ridiculed at anyone's expense. I don't ever remember signing up to be lied to, talked about, used and abused by anyone. However, I now know and fully understand that this came with the package, and until that final season was over, I would have to learn how to become steadfast and unmovable in God, no matter what.

The more I grew in God, the more there were times when I felt that my very life, along with my spouse, was under a mini-microscope. There were some who attempted to mock us, formed their opinions, lied to us, and wished us harm on so many levels. Occasionally, we were falsely accused about things that we were never guilty of, but no one took the real time to examine the truth because that wasn't their real purpose in the first place.

I would like to go on record and say that this was not the consensus of everyone; it never really is, but for those who were very good at lying and backbiting, they often made the lie almost look like the truth. Thank God I am very acquainted with myself and know the truth from a setup.

What I was noticing among all the trials and tribulations was that God was still in control over my life, circumstances, and my situations and that He was still using me and my ministry for His glory, even in the midst of my private, and sometimes very public, pain. I realized while being in the middle of the heat of the spiritual furnace that I was also right in the middle of the will and purpose of the Almighty God for my life as well. Yes, the heat was being turned up, but God was in control of the thermostat all the while.

In fact, when my husband and I lived in San Antonio, Texas, I worked for this particular law firm where the gentleman was Jewish. The first things that he told me when I started working for him were (1) "I don't like your Jesus," and (2) "I don't particularly care for black people." I said to him, "Well, you must be color-blind, because I am guilty on all fronts! And I am going to still need to keep my job!" Seriously, even though he was a fruit cake ready to be baked, I knew that God had once again handpicked me for another special assignment. Yes, you are correct, it wasn't easy; but somebody had to do it. It should not come as a surprise to anyone when I say this: he did not make it easy on me at all. I served my time well while being in the prison of my employment there. I often looked forward to getting my get-out- of-jail-free card. In fact, one day after crying out to God, I decided to ask the Lord about why my walk with Him was so tumultuous, and His response to me was, *"Because, you are most effective to me in the fire!"* Not being exactly sure about what that statement meant, I inquired further, Are you saying that I am not saved?

And I got this reply: *There are some people who are content with just being lukewarm or close to the fire but not directly involved or connected to the fire. But you I can use directly in the fire, and I know that you will give me your best praise.*

In essence, God is most interested in building up his Kingdom with those of us who are willing to step up to the task and maintain their post until their assignments are completed in Christ Jesus, while there are too many others who are entirely too content with others doing all the work whether it's within the church walls or outside in the hedges and byways. Still, there are others who just show up for guest appearances when the true labor of it all is finished.

I continued to flow in Innovative Ministry and watched God continuously perform great and marvelous things in that vein for the ministry itself and through His people. I observed as God supernaturally opened doors and closed some necessary ones that were long overdue for spiritual maintenance and renewal.

I distinctively remember how He ushered in new and refreshed friendships and restored some old relationships, all the while compelling me to move forward in His name. Along the way, He encouraged and coached me into the right seasons at the right time, every step of the way requiring monumental faith and trust in His name. Occasionally, along the way, God would remind me that not all fruit mature in the same season. That's why it is vital that everyone examine their personal fruit, paying close attention to the expectation date of maturity or manifestation.

For the one who sows to his own flesh will from the flesh reap corruption, but the one who sows to the Spirit will from the Spirit reap eternal life. Let us not lose heart in doing good, for in due time we will reap if we do not grow weary. So then, while we have opportunity, let us do good to all people, and especially to those who are of the household of the faith. (Gal. 6:9)

When others discovered that I was surviving without them, some protested even louder: "How is she going to make it without us?" There were some who refused to sup - port the conferences and told others as well not to attend. I remember on one specific occasion, after one of the conferences, this particular person asked me, "Sister Brenda, how was the conference? Was Jesus there?" To which I replied with my quick wit, "Would you recognize Him if He were?"

Honestly, by now, I was so over people and their limited imagination and their perception of who they thought their god was to me. At this point in my journey, it didn't mat-ter who I was being sold out by, kicked out by, or talked about by. All I knew now was that I had deliberately and intentionally decided that I was going to continue to follow Jesus wherever He led me, and that there would be absolutely no turning back or around. I was moving forward in His name regardless of who supported, boycotted, or staged a protest or what have you. I declared I was victorious in Jesus's name, and I was content to stay with the One who continuously looked out and presided over my soul and my daily needs.

In August 2008, after leaving the job I had held for eight years, I was dreading the unknown. I wondered how God was going to get glory from my departure there. Daily, I would write in my personal journal and date the conversations so that I could have a paper trail of how incredible God's hand would move in and over my life in the coming days, weeks, and even months, ahead.

When I would often give my testimony that I was no longer

employed, some people would say, "Oh my God, did you really lose your job?" I would say, "No, I didn't lose it. It is in the same place I left it off of 820 East and Collins exit." I have just completed that assignment, and God is moving me forward to another one.

The truth of the matter was I hadn't realized that working in any call center environment was stressful to the hundredth level. It is demanding, taxing, and pulls life out of you. While some of the customers were demanding, needy, threatening, hostile, and ruthless, surprisingly, others were very kind, professional, patient, and even knowledgeable about their account information. Needless to say, thank God for the deliverance!

In the thick of things, leaving that job was one of the best options for me. Not only did I get some much-needed rest and relaxation, but I was better able to put important and necessary things into proper perspective for my household and my life.

I hadn't realized it yet, but I later learned that, in the process of it all, my God was going to use that very pain to thrust me into my next purpose. Now, here I was, with-out employment but still desiring to do ministry full-time, which required some form of income. I relied on Him for the gas money, lunch money, hair appointment money, nails, and pedicures—well, you get the gist of where I am going with all this…

As time progressed, I inquired of a true friend about a specific dream I had the night before the final decision came relating to my employment with my company. In the dream, I was out of town on business, and one evening, while I was there, I went outside to move my car to keep it from being towed, and I encountered this gigantic snake. In fact, it wasn't just any old snake, but it was described as a python. Pythons are specific in nature. They are described as being large, primitive snakes of tropical Asian and African nature.

According to eHow,

The python is not poisonous. However, it can inflict a severe wound with its many long, sharp teeth. It eats birds and mammals, capturing its prey by biting and holding on, and then swiftly looping its body around the victim. The snake tightens its coils until the prey, unable to breathe, dies of suffocation.

As I was moving my car in the dream, I didn't notice the snake hiding out in the bushes waiting to bite me. When I turned around to go back into the hotel, I heard a noise and looked down, and the snake was already in position to strike, and strike he did on the back of my head. I could literally hear and seemingly feel the bones crushing from the pressure of its bite.

Blood was oozing down from the back of my skull; and as I turned to look at it, the snake was gazing directly into my eyes with my blood coming out of its mouth and I said to the face of it that was revealed to me, "Oh my God, I never would have thought it would have been you." The snake smiled and said, "I finally got you." And I woke up.

Within 24 hours of that specific dream, I was let go from a place of business where I had never once been written up, I had never even received any type of warning, or received any negative feedback.

Up until then, I had always received outstanding reviews, bonuses, and promotions left and right. What changed, you ask? Three days prior to being dismissed, I was asked to take another supervisor's shift in interviewing potential new employees for that afternoon.

Mind you, each supervisor had a day of interviewing no matter what else we had to do. However, that was not the case daily. If others didn't feel like it or simply didn't want to carry out their duties, they would make excuses, disappear off the floor, or just got their manager involved with finding others to take their place.

Well, after being off the floor for eight hours interviewing the day before, I was summoned to continue the grueling process of interviewing the next day. The second person that I interviewed that day was a young woman who was very nice and cheery in spirit. As we began to chat, she began to tell me that she was moving to Texas from another state and that her father had just passed, and she became visibly upset to the point where we had to stop the interview for a while.

Being that my dad had recently passed away, I felt the sting of not having one and could relate to her obvious pain. Offering her words of encouragement, I shared some scriptures with her, and she asked about what church I was attending, and I simply passed on that information to her and continued with the interview.

A few minutes later, someone from Human Resources entered the room and became upset because the interview process had not progressed as quickly as she had hoped and went back and complained to this particular manager, who, little did I know, was just waiting for an opportunity to write me up and, apparently, fire me. Armed with this information, this was his, or their, opportunity to do so.

Just a side bar: while working for this company, approximately 80 to 85 percent of all the employees—along with various supervisors, managers, and directors included— have at some point come to me on several occasions for prayer, consultation, advice, direction, and clarity.

They knew I was a Christian, and that I wholeheartedly loved Jesus and that it was a fact. And while I didn't walk into the call center carrying my big King James Version Bible, or any other version of the Bible, to preach a sermon, or hold Bible studies in the aisle, they knew this was my walk because they often inquired of it daily, weekly, and/or monthly, including the one who was desperate to fire me.

Overnight, the Lord made clear to me the repercussions of my doing and the outcome of it all. I was encouraged to talk to a specific friend about this situation, because I knew that God used her in the realm of the prophetic word. True to form, I called her the next day, and whereas it is usually difficult to contact her during working hours, that day, when I called her, she readily answered her phone as though she was specifically waiting for my call. I shared with her all that God had placed on my heart.

She immediately prayed with me and began to instruct me to go back into the building and not to worry. That the outcome of what I had previously done would be what I had been told by God; however, I was to be assured that it was the will of God, and that not too many days henceforth after my release from prison—I apologize, my employment—I would get the answer to why it was necessary to depart under such terms. While I would not be there to receive the news, the news would seek me out in the process.

After reentering the building, the enemy immediately descended upon me as though I was an intruder from a third world country traveling through the United States without a proper or updated visa. I was approached by my immediate supervisor and told to come into our boss's office. I was literally interrogated and badgered for a minimum of two hours.

I could tell from my immediate boss's face that it wasn't his idea; this deliberate setup was orchestrated by the enemy who took great pride in his actions. This person always prided himself on being in a certain role within the company and a certain level that he had achieved all by himself. He often bragged about being the director of the call center and how he had worked hard to get there. Not understanding why he was about to blow a private gasket about something that wasn't even negative, I chose to settle myself and listened to what he had to say.

As the director began to speak, it was obvious that he was angry, proud, puffed up, confused, and definitely full of himself; and with the little evidence he had and was supposedly holding over my head, he zoomed in for the kill. I got the strongest impression that he somehow wanted me to beg, plead, and cry for mercy to keep my job, to which he would have the pleasure of saying no anyway.

The calmer I remained, the more out of control he became. He began sweating, swearing at times, talking fast, and repeating sentences that didn't apply to the current conversation or situation. You know, lying and underhanded work will do that to you; however, I think they may have medication now on the market for this type of behavior, but don't quote me on that one.

He told me not once or twice, but three different times, how the young woman valued and appreciated my consoling her and encouragement. She raved about it being one of the best interviews she had ever experienced. She thanked me for my compassion and humanness during our inter-view; and whether or not she got the job, she was able to walk out confident that she would gain employment sooner rather than later.

After my supervisor told me this information, he yelled at me and said, "Now, do you see how you have crossed the line? This type of behavior will not be tolerated in our workplace. I am ashamed of you, you are considered a seasoned employee and you have totally crossed the line by ministering to this woman while on the job. This is, quite frankly, unacceptable behavior."

He is ashamed of me? Really, while daily there were senior managers sleeping with, dating, shacking up with, and harassing others who were on their teams but not of the same seniority or interests, or even the same sex were ever chastised. There were people walking around with their pants so low on their rears if I didn't know any better, I could have mistaken them for a mini skirt—all that was missing were the stilettos, and they were never written up for this behavior? Are you serious?

Oftentimes, the rap music and everyday drama of people fighting in the building, parking lot, bathroom, cursing, stealing, cheating, being unprofessional to the customers and their peers—and through all of that, you could only surmise that I was acting unprofessional for ministering to another person who gave me glowing reviews.

During the time of my exit interview, I was met by the Human Resources Department where my boss and the woman I was speaking with were both crying and saying that they had no idea why this was happening to me and that they were just "following orders." The meeting became so awkward I ended up consoling and counseling them for the last time.

Not sure as to how I would feel after this meeting, when I walked through the final doors, as the sunlight and wind touched my skin, honestly, I felt alive, vibrant, and instantly, life reentered my body. I felt delivered, rejuvenated, and set free from bondage and the enemy's trap. I all but ran across the parking lot—first, in a true praise and worship, and secondly knowing that I didn't have to return to this prison, ever again.

As I walked to my car, tears of joy streamed down my face, and I realized just how much the Lord loved me as he was delivering me from the snares of the fowler. That day, He had in fact, tamed and/or wired the mouths of the lions and demons that were deliberately set out to destroy me through stress and being overloaded with my workload.

Coming into work early and staying late due to the call volume and others calling in or running late for their shifts, being forced to be on call even when I finally had a weekend off, or receiving calls to come in at a moment's notice. Other days working through breaks and lunches, and some days the lack of lunch coverage and so on...The more I thought about my "temporary" situation, I began to rejoice and shout "Hallelujah to the Newborn King!" This is a good day that the Lord has made, I was definitely going to rejoice and be extremely glad in it.

After this experience, I went back to school and completed my bachelor's degree and began to set my sights on greater meaning for my life. Not only did I complete my degree, but I did so with honors! Little did I know that God was teaching me something much greater than I had ever experienced before in my personal walk with Him—

and that was to learn to trust Him explicitly! Do not look to the left or to the right, and certainly, not to lean unto my own understanding.

Even though I had great job interviews with various companies, I now understand that those positions were not where the Lord wanted me to go, and therefore, those doors were not opened to me. Believe it or not, during my last three interviews, I never received a "no" from any of the positions, just not now. Even though I didn't under-stand it then, and sometimes had difficulty accepting those responses, God was teaching and grooming me in the realm of raw faith.

Eventually, one day I was working on my homework at home, and I suddenly felt the prompting from the leader-ship of the Holy Spirit to go downtown Fort Worth to a job fair at this hotel that was being built. I did so, but after arriving, there were no parking spaces close by, so I found myself having to walk about four to five blocks. I was not happy about this at all.

Not only that, the place looked a mess; there was debris everywhere in the street, construction work and dust in the air, traffic going in both directions and seemingly chaos everywhere I looked. I not only had second thoughts, but third, fourth, and fifth. In fact, walking almost halfway there, I started twice to turn around and go back home and burn rubber while doing so.

After finally finding the building and entering, I saw no one. I heard no one in the building. It was quiet as a mouse. I thought, *What is this? Did I get the directions wrong? Was the job fair cancelled? What's really going on?*

Being there for over two hours completing an application, waiting to be interviewed, and getting the necessary feedback took its toll on me. Finally, I was called by this woman who spoke extremely quietly. She had what appeared to be this permanent smile on her face and was very rigid during our one-minute interview. Looking at her, all I could remember about her interview was her very soft voice, a sea of humongous diamonds, and the one precious minute we spent together.

Shortly after my name was called, she took me back to her station, introduced herself, shook my hand, and offered me a seat. She looked me directly in the eyes, leaned for-ward, and said, "Now, Brenda, I'll just tell you now, I will not be hiring you as an administrative person, although it is clear that you can type and do computer work. I am going to recommend that you be placed somewhere out in the open where others will be able to see you and gain access to you."

Little could she have known that was a negative on all accounts: not only did I not want to be seen and/or be accessible, I wasn't necessarily in a hurry to meet and greet the public again as well. Nevertheless, she continued, "You have a light within you that doesn't belong hidden, and I am not going to hire you to work behind some desk, where it will not be able to shine through."

With that, she stood up, smiled at me and directed me to follow her back to the room we had just left. She said I should hear from her directly within a couple of weeks. I was literally mortified. I honestly could not believe my ears or my eyes. I asked myself what in the world just happened to me. Was she kidding? When I tried to protest, she just thanked me and turned and walked away. I left that place highly upset and dejected and utterly confused. I thought she has surely lost her ever loving mind. When I arrived back at my car, I had a ticket from the parking meter, sore feet and a long, slow drive back home, great! Just what I lived for…

On the way home, I began to complain that I was never, ever going to take a job from this hotel, and that if, or should, they call, I would, in fact, tell them so. For days after, I was furious about my time being wasted and wished I had never allowed myself to be humiliated in that manner. Three weeks later, while at home alone, my phone rang, and it was this individual calling me again and inquiring about me being ready to start my new venture.

I did not pick up the phone, but, rather, choose to mock her message for me. The more she began to leave me specific directions about when I was supposed to start, what I was to wear, parking, etc., I am in the background giving her the silent *What for?* I am throwing my hands up in the air, protesting loudly, "No, I am not, no I am not!" Now I realize that God was probably saying, "Yes, you are! Yes, you are!"

She kept calling and calling, eventually wearing me down. I finally answered the phone and said to her, "Thank you for the call, but I am going to decline the offer," ever so nicely and professionally.

In reply, the woman, said to me, "Brenda, our next class is starting on December 29, 2009. May I please put you down for it?"

I thought, *Is this person nuts, did she not hear what I just said?* I started looking around my home, checking for cameras, phone tapping, police officers, or anything out of the ordinary. *What's really going on?*

We ended the call, and she kept calling nonstop for the next several days. After consulting with at least three different people that I trusted about my strange interview and what direction I should take, everyone said that I should just go with it. I was taken aback, because I thought they all had lost their everlasting minds too. Didn't anyone see that I was overqualified for this role—and not only that, that I was not interested in standing on my feet for eight and a half hours a day?

Eventually, I took the job; and when I showed up for the actual assignment, it was something that I absolutely never, ever would have dreamed of in a million years. I was working in Starbucks, with the first assignment of helping to put together the actual outlet from scratch. You see, the hotel was still under major construction, and all of the employees had to attend new employee orientation for six hours and help put the outlets together for the remainder of the day.

In order to do that, we all had to wear yellow hardhats, goggles, an orange -and- yellow highway vest, boots, and gloves. I just knew: Lord, this cannot be you at all! Not only had I missed the vision for my life, but the heavenly computer screen must have been all the way down because this cannot be my life. I thought, Absolutely no way is this possible.

Needless to say, I protested, complained, cried, kicked, screamed, and threatened to quit daily. I felt as though I was in an out-of-body experience, made and taken over by aliens for which some days I was very grateful because at least I did not have to endure unnecessary pain for that particular moment. You talking about Jesus, please, take the wheel… well, I was ready for him to upgrade the entire vehicle!

For the next several weeks, we were in hot pursuit of training and getting ready to open the building in record time. For the grand opening! The trainer was very demanding, loud, focused, and driven. Honestly, I believe this woman could lift at least eight small midgets with one hand and never break a sweat. She was fierce, and packing a troublesome attitude to boot! Whatever she said, we little weaklings were found struggling trying to get the job done—absolutely no questions asked!

Because of the oversight on when the building should actually open, our training sessions were cut back from thirteen weeks to six. Within that time frame, we had to work while it was day and learn how to make twenty-five different drink mixes, including shakes, hot drinks, and smoothies within the next couple of weeks, which concluded with our certifications—all within a span of three weeks. After sniffing, taste-testing, and eating coffee beans every day, well, I will just say that those were some of the best nights of sleep I may have gotten in a long time. Do you suppose the beans had anything to do with it, or, quite possibly, the extra espresso shots? I'm just saying.

During this process, we were asked to introduce our-selves to the team. I didn't want to know anyone, and I didn't particularly care for them to know my name or any-thing about me either. After all, in my mind, it wouldn't matter; I was not planning on staying around that long. All I was looking for out of this job was merely twenty hours of workweek, working with the customers and getting to meet different people, free drinks, and an opportunity to stay at the hotel at a significantly discounted rate. Other than that, it was not my immediate choice of a career move or movement.

So when it was my turn to introduce myself, I made sure that I told them the very minimum about me and hurried up and sat down. Of all the things to say, the group leader said to me, "So what church do you go to?" No one else was asked that particular question at all. I took a deep breath, paused, and tried to gather my bearings and I said, "Excuse me, did you ask me what church I attended?" She said, "Yes, did you not understand me?" I could not understand why out of eight other employees, most of whom looked sane and intelligent, I was the only one being asked the question.

I got brave enough to pose the question, "Why am I the only one being asked this question?" To my surprise, the woman said, "Everyone in here already knows that you are a Christian. We can see it all over you. Now, what church do you attend? We want to know."

I almost fainted right then and there—not because I was a Christian but where in the world was this coming from, and what was the purpose of this anyway?

Of course I told her, but I was curious as to why I was asked that particular question when no one else in the group was. The training that was supposed to last for thirteen weeks was now cut down again to a mere four. It was sheer overload and pandemonium at best.

When the doors opened for business, we were all terrified. Daily, the lines were wrapped around the entire building; and on most days, we had doubled lines inside the hotel lobby. I was the shyest one in the bunch, but was the one thrown to the wolves at the cash register, taking orders for the grand opening. Not only did I not know what a Venti meant, but a Grande was equally confusing. It seemed as though the customer's took pride in speaking a hundred words per minute in giving their orders.

I'm sure the look on my face said Really, people? Thank God I was an experienced prayer warrior, because every bit of training came into play over the next several months. People would scream, curse, became belligerent and utterly out of control when you didn't speak their Starbucks language. I knew that I needed to have a daily out-of-body experience in order to quickly be able to take their order, serve their drinks correctly—and this had to be done all while greeting them with an angelic smile.

The more I realized that unless I learned how to sing praise songs fluently, dance in the spirit, speak in tongues, and get a Word from the Lord, I most likely would be heading for the big house—and not the mansions located in Colleyville or someplace extravagant but someplace in a cute, chic little straitjacket.

Absolutely no one, including my boss, wanted any part of the meet-and-greet, the cash register, or anything up front. They all ran to the back, and it took eight of them to figure out a simple cup order. While I will admit that I was extremely nervous, I could not understand why all eight of them were shaking in their boots. At least they were all standing together. There I was, standing there unprotected and alone. Hoping for the sheer best….

Daily I prayed, moaned, groaned, cried, and even tried once or twice to bribe God into releasing me from Egypt. No such luck. My then supervisor was anything but a viable leader, and it became very apparent that this leadership role was way out of her league in leading others in an establishment of this magnitude, and the entire staff suffered as a result of it too.

Through it all, God was teaching me patience, endurance, perseverance, longsuffering, and perhaps how to stay out of any uniforms pertaining to black-and-white pinstripes, orange or taupe colors! Seriously, though, once I got over myself and worrying about what others thought of me, including church folks, I was better for it.

My experience as a barista wasn't entirely bad. In fact, while spending my spiritual time in the incubator of my next level ministry,

I now understand that this was the very best place for me. I grew under much ridged scrutiny and micro -management by each manager. With the time spent at the hotel and eight managers later, and to my surprise, I was still standing.

Although I was intensely aware and familiar with stress and stressful moments, this was a new and improved level for me. I was tested in every way possible. Other employees would steal from my cash register or steal from monies left in my apron. Some wouldn't show up for work on time, or at all. Breaks would often be overlooked because the store had to be protected at all times. It was a very unique, wild experience. Not one day went by without some serious challenges, to say the least…but God!

I witnessed all types of crazy things—couples breaking up and making up in the lobby, fistfights breaking out among visitors, employees' jealous boyfriends coming up to the store, people having side-bar relationships with other employees while on the job, you name it, I probably witnessed it firsthand. I was chosen for the earliest shift that began at 5:00 a.m. That meant that I needed to be up at three o'clock each morning and in the car by 4:15 a.m. and on my way to work.

When the hotel first opened, its employees were given a specific place to park. Good luck with all that, because that meant it would be first come and first served. This meant that we could have been parking, walking, jogging, standing right next to Mr. Bobo, who may have just gotten out of jail and just happened to be downtown at 4:15 a.m. as well.

It was inevitable that some days required that I would have to park in what I called Egypt and walk across the Jordan, which was every bit about six blocks away from my destination. Can you imagine walking at four fifteen in the cold, dark, sometimes rainy, eerie, and dangerous mornings by yourself—except I knew that Jesus was with me, and even before me, because I live to tell about it.

One day, while sweeping the hotel lobby, there was this

particular police officer along with one of my bosses who complimented me on how clean my apron and uniform always looked. I thanked them both and kept it moving. However, when I went to count my drawer out for the day, the officer noticed my pepper spray and inquired with my boss why I had it on the floor with me. So naturally, my then boss wanted to know my purpose for it as well. When I explained that it was for protection, he said, "Now, you know you should not be carrying pepper spray with you on the premises. Why did you do that?"

I looked them both in their faces and said, "I am sorry, sirs. I guess it could be the fact that when I get up at 3:00 a.m. and get dressed and walk out the door at 4:15 a.m. to stroll through the dangerous parks, highways, and byways, mingling with the murderers, rapists, prisoners, and the like, perhaps I just keep it for safety measures just in case. I don't want to be robbed or worse that day." After all, I wouldn't want to disturb others while they are at home sleeping in their warm, comfortable beds next to their significant others.

Over time, I learned how to adapt to the environment and prayed, fasted, fought, cried, and sang my way through. Truly the presence of the Lord was there. After six months of employment, I still did not like my job, nor did I enjoy working there because it was forever evolving and changing from morning, noon, and even night; however, little by little, I started to believe that there was a method to this madness. I started to believe that it was an assignment that I was being placed in, and that once I learned how to listen to God and obey Him, I was going to be blessed in the process of it all.

This all meant that I had to surrender in a way and method that was different to and for me. No matter what, I was to surrender my will, purpose, plan, desires, and goals unto God and allow Him to direct my path. I definitely could not walk around all day being engulfed with my emotions all across the place, feelings being easily challenged, or blown away by every wind or doctrine. This would take some incredible faith, trust, and resilience on my part, sometimes in a moment's notice.

As if the job was not challenging enough, I was selected to work from 5:00 a.m. until sometimes 6:00 p.m., because most of the staff would not show up to work, period. Because of the out-of-control crowds, we would be overlooked for breaks and lunches and expected to continuously provide A+ service, nonstop.

My shift was always from Monday morning until sometimes Saturday evening nonstop. Everyone wanted the tips, but no one wanted the labor or the hours. The group I originally started with was very young, 18 to 21 years of age. It's funny now; however, that was not always the case then. But I remember most days being on the shift with a young woman who had just graduated from high school.

Her idea of being on time for work was getting there three hours after her shift had started. In fact, she could be found calling in three to four hours after her shift started and telling the supervisor that she would be in a little late: "I am running just a little bit behind." And when she did show up for work, she took delight in flirting with all the male customers and inquiring about how much of the tip money she should collect. Wow, those were the days!

Over time, I met some wonderful and memorable people. There are some that I will never forget how much they truly meant to me in that time and space. After a while, I looked forward to serving and fellowshipping with my customers. They had become like family, and we often encouraged each other to move forward, enjoy life, and to be grateful for each and every moment.

I met this very special customer by the name of J. Rodgers, who was a little rough around the edges; however, he was really a cream puff once you got to know him. J. Rodgers would frequent the store and give us advice about specific things we needed to improve upon, whether you asked him or not. Most of us ran in the opposite direction when they saw him coming (because they were so intimidated by him); they didn't want to risk looking or saying something that would embarrass themselves.

While I didn't know him either, I sensed that he was a person of special interest, and one that over time I could learn a great deal from. Indeed, over time, I did. Later, I was introduced to his beautiful wife, Bettye, who has an infectious smile and laughter. Bettye is extremely wise in her business affairs and genuine in her friendships. I am always intrigued by how she holds it all together—business, social life, personal life, and life in general.

I call her a friend because I can see her heart a mile away; and to me, she is always the same: first the beautiful smile, then the arms stretched out to embrace me, and she always ended our conversation with "I love you." Cannot get any better than that. I am so thankful for the place she holds in my life.

Additionally, people came and went—employees, man-agers, and customers—but the Lord allowed me to minister to the masses without fail. Before long, I enjoyed hearing God speaking and ministering through me to others, as well as receiving the blessing of Him ministering to me through others. During those years of working for the hotel, my income shifted quite significantly from the managerial level of pay that I was accustomed to making. In fact, while working at the hotel, for about six months, I didn't even open my paycheck. I just literally decided to tithe the entire amount to the church because I knew that whatever amount that was on the stub was not going to be enough to sustain what I needed to take care of things for my household.

Daily, or at least paydays, I would whisper to the Lord, "God, I thank you for this income. Although I am not happy, I choose to believe that you will provide for me and my every need. Please provide a miracle check to take care of my financial needs and monthly responsibilities."

While I didn't receive a big fat pay raise after the prayer, I did witness the Lord daily providing that extra income through my tips and other means. God is, and will always remain, faithful when we trust Him with our all.

Little by little, I began to witness change in my personal walk with Christ. I was being changed and renewed in my mind as it related to my thinking. I witnessed God creating new ways and adventures for me and my ministry. I could see His hands opening new doors and windows on my behalf. I saw countless favors given me in ways I could not imagine or explain, all because of His goodness toward me.

Lives of God's people were being changed right before my very eyes, and there were those who accepted Christ on the spot while purchasing a cup of coffee on the bases of just sheer conversation and allowing my life and light to shine before men that they may see Jesus through my surrendering spirit. There were some men, women, and even young teenagers, who gave their lives while waiting for their orders to be completed. To God be the glory!

In fact, on such special occasions, there was this gentleman—he was my director who was of Indian descent, and he told me once that he did not believe in God and that his family was so poor and he couldn't imagine that any kind of God of love, joy, or goodness existed because of the personal oppression he witnessed in his village as a little boy. His father was strict. He began working at a very, very young age and had to drop out of school to help his family financially. Still, his dad expected him to do great things in the world.

By the time he had reached the United States, he was angry, bitter and desperate to find his own way without the help of any God in sight—at least that was what he thought. As I got to know my director, I found he had a very strong personality and a very heavy hand in ruling over others in the way of leadership. Whatever he said, there were no questions or hesitation about the matter; all he cared about first and foremost was getting things done, and quickly.

He rarely smiled, and at all times, talked in a very authoritative manner to all of his subordinates. There were many who hated him. They would rather beg for food than to have him be their supervisor.

When he showed up for work, everyone would scatter and pretend that they didn't see him for fear he would yell at them or write them up.

Even on your best day, your work was never good enough. He would write people up or simply fire them without notice or with little room for error. One day, he came into Starbucks and said, "Hey you, what's your name?" I told him, and he said, "You're fired!" I gladly said, "Okay, let me get my purse." And I ran as quickly as my size 8.5 shoes could carry me, thinking Blessed feet of God, today is your day of great escape. Feet, don't fail me now!

With a big smile on my face and purse in hand, I was going around the counter when he stopped me before reaching the door and said, "Where do you think you are going?" My reply was, "Home, James, home." He didn't think that was funny at all. In fact, he ordered me to get back to work until he said that I could go home. When I challenged him on the fact that he had just fired me, he said, "Well then, you still cannot leave until after your shift is over."

I was always, always reciting a scripture reference, all the time not realizing that he was noticing or curious as to what I was really saying. Little did I know that he was taking personal notes and going home and looking up the scripture references I was using and finding and studying other various scripture references to challenge me for our next encounter.

I was not only impressed with his Bible knowledge, but daily, I witnessed his entire life changing for the better. His demeanor, his attitude toward his employees, his patience with us, and that he was now starting to speak and tell jokes from time to time. Before long, we were both growing in the Lord and learning how to be an encourager to others, as well as a source of light for each other.

After about a year of walking in this new lifestyle, my friend's boss started to treat him in a very derogatory manner. He would yell and belittle him in front of his peers. His boss would give him last-minute projects to complete, which meant his shift would now be extended without extra pay. My friend's boss would pretend that he could not remember whether or not he was given a specific task to complete for that day, or the boss would simply change his daily work shift at the last minute.

After the second year of the hotel opening, my friend received one of the highest ratings and awards a director could get, and this did not go well in the eyes of his boss. After my friend received the recognition, his boss took away his raise, demoted him, and shortened his hours with-out any notice whatsoever.

This was not only appalling and unscrupulous for my friend, but he was hurt and embarrassed, to say the least. He was also very angry and wanted to let his boss and Human Resources know exactly how he felt. He asked me what he should do and how he should handle the situation. We agreed to fast and pray about the problem and believe that God would reveal the correct answer in due season.

During this particular time, our city had been experiencing some challenging weather storms, specifically with tornados hovering in the area. It seemed as though every day for that entire week, we were being inundated with threats of either severe weather storms or a tornado touching down in surrounding counties, with little to no warning.

On this particular evening, after I arrived home, I just so happened to have the news on, which I hardly ever do, and I caught a glimpse of the Dallas news. The station was in the middle of giving the weather report from downtown Dallas. Interestingly, as the news was being broadcast live from downtown Dallas, the commentator had no idea that a tornado was being spotted right over his head, with a funnel cloud hanging down in the background while he was filming.

While the sky was dark, windy, gloomy, on one side of the street, the sun was shining in the distance. The tornado was looming over cars, people, buildings, etc.; and every-one below was totally oblivious about its presence looming directly over their heads. I thought, Wow, are these people nuts? Could they not tell that there was something happening right above their heads? Couldn't they sense danger lurking?

In an instant, I was reminded of my friend's situation and what he had just gone through. During my friend's conversation with me, he had reiterated over and over how he didn't see this coming, and how could he have been so blind-sided in the midst of it all? In my prayer time with the Lord about his situation, it was revealed to me that it wasn't that he was blind-sided, but just like the people who were in trouble underneath the tornado and funnel cloud didn't notice the danger lurking up ahead, God still protected them nonetheless.

I informed my friend the next day that just like those innocent people traveling and going about their daily routine without a care in the world, God protected him and allowed him to continue to perform an excellent job in what his hands were assigned to: serving the people, keeping everything on point, opening and closing the restaurant on time. Even though the enemy was working behind the scenes to discredit his name and his accomplishments, God had crossed ahead of him and was making his crooked ways plain.

When the time would come for him to move forward to greater promotions and opportunities, God would lead the way and empower him to do what he needed to do, and he would arrive on time and on schedule. Armed with that information, my friend held his head up, squared his shoulders, and decided to move forward. You could see life return to his being. He was assured that God would take care of him and his family.

Lo and behold! Within two weeks' time, my friend had received his answer and proceeded to forge ahead without hesitation. He scheduled an appointment with his boss and gave him his two weeks' notice. To his surprise, his boss became enraged, but accepted his resignation. Before leaving to move out of state, he thanked me for being his friend and showing him Jesus. Because of our daily biblical verse exchanges, he was eagerly reading his Bible daily, praying and placing his trust and hope in the hands of the Lord.

My friend moved to New Orleans, where he was promoted at another great restaurant. He and his wife have welcomed a baby girl into their lives and have since moved back to the Grand Prairie area, where they bought a home. My friend has planned to further his education by enrolling into Texas Christian University (TCU) in the summer or fall. He has never looked back. When God closes one door, He is more than qualified to open another.

Daily, the Lord used me to minister to countless of people—perhaps the majority of them I will never encounter again in this life, but by taking full advantage of the opportunities afforded to me in the moment, that meant the world to me.

In each instance, raw faith taught me about leaning into God and diving into His presence without full knowledge and total understanding of just how He alone was going to bring me out, fix, solve, or handle the problem or circumstance, knowing that the greatest lesson learned in the trial is one that I will learn about myself, and not necessarily how it would change others.

Raw faith for me is more about taking my previous experiences and using them as frontlets and directional guards for my way out of what can sometimes be a dire circumstance or situation, at least to me. Raw faith has taught me how to become calm in raging waters. How to literally speak to my storms and cause them, through faith, to cease. I have learned how to ride on the wings of the wind as opposed to being tossed and turned in the turbulence of it all.

I now am assured that the absolute safest place in the midst of a horrible storm is directly in the eye of it where traces of Jesus resides. I am confident that Our God never sleeps or slumbers while we are being affected by various issues because He alone is always in control.

~ Now Faith ~

*Faith is the confidence that what we hope for will actually happen;
it gives us assurance about things we cannot see.
—Hebrews 11:1 (NLT)*

Faith to me is choosing to believe in something much bigger than I can dream and imagine. It is the essence by which I dream and wait for. It's my desire hidden in confidential form. I embrace faith in such a manner that lets me personally know that while I understand in and of myself, I cannot make anything happen; however, when I choose to dream big, remain focused, and do the work by applied muscle to my faith in God resting in Him being fully persuaded that in due season, He alone will bring it to pass.

Faith to me is what I am privileged to see in the spiritual realm only through the lens of the Almighty God about my situation, circumstances, hopes, and my dreams. Faith speaks in such a manner to my will, desires, and purposes that it compels me to move toward what I have a glimpse of even when I don't have the means, motive, or method to make it happen on my own.

Faith stirs my soul into believing that with God, all things are just possible. It will not allow me to rest until actions are put forth. My faith is a stirring beyond my comprehension. My personal faith is not ordinary, but rather, it causes the extraordinary to become transformed out of my ordinary situations. My faith challenges me to throw caution to the wind. It beckons me to move beyond stagnation, retardation, and hesitation into the divine purpose, plan, and provision that Jesus has already paid for.

My faith requires me, as an individual, to embrace those things that are ahead of me and choosing to forget about those things that are behind me. My faith pushes me to stop focusing on dead things in my life that are no longer applicable, necessary, or at the very least, nonfunctional to my journey. It encourages me to not give any of my energy to what's on the sidelines, or even what may or may not ever happen in my life. My faith has a way of staying me when my knees have a tendency to buckle beneath the personal cares of this world. It causes me to keep it moving in the wake of adversity at the highest level.

My faith produces through labor, diligence, perseverance, trial, and testing that I can do all things through Christ who strengthens me. Faith causes me to believe the impossible, reach beyond the norm of what I can see, expect or think. My faith pulls out of me what I did not realize I had in me, until I found myself dealing with undue and sudden pressures, not only from outside forces but inside ones as well. Even still, God stayed His hands over my life and my circumstances.

Through my faith, it produces a sense of staying power that can eradicate the biggest lie, setback, hold up, and delay concerning my deliverance. Daily, I am learning that through my faith it can move me over every obstacle, it stops for no negative lingo, it knows no unnecessary boundaries, and it certainly does not answer to any critics or criticism. In fact, it is through my faith that I am persuaded that once I have received divine revelation from on high, absolutely nothing can shut down the mind of my personal faith.

Not only can my faith boost my confidence to move me forward and challenge me to finish what God has started in me, but my faith serves as a capable vehicle to make sure that I arrive on time and on schedule. Through my faith, I am capable of demonstrating to the world that even when I am being persecuted, I can have the godly assurance that I am not being forsaken. When my soul is being temporarily cast down, I know beyond a shadow of a doubt that I am not destroyed.

> *That even being confronted with my present situations and circumstances....For our present troubles are small and won't last very long. Yet they produce for us a glory that vastly outweighs them and will last forever. So we don't look at the troubles we can see now; rather, we fix our gaze on things that cannot be seen. For the things we see now will soon be gone, but the things we cannot see will last forever. (2 Cor. 4:9, 4:17–18)*

Faith teaches me that nothing that stands before me today, this hour, right now is beyond immovable when it's placed directly in the hands of the Almighty God. I am utterly convinced that the God I serve can, and is well able and qualified to, cause all things to work together for my good and my purpose; He will not allow any weapon that raises itself against me to prosper in any manner.

My faith does not allow me to cater to my innermost fears, anxieties, pressures, concerns, fright, circumstances, situations, or to be overwhelmed because of them. My faith is unstoppable under pressure because I am learning to keep my eyes on the deal breaker, Jesus, and not on limited personal weaknesses. Through Christ, my faith knows no boundaries or limitations because in Christ, I recognize that in God there are absolutely no failures. My faith is that substance which I call the residue or the residuals of what it will look like when it is all over with.

My faith is the substance (the outcome) of what I have been in labor with during the duration of my waiting period.

It is the object of which I have set my mind, heart, and soul upon that teaches me if I remain in the state of faith, I will deliver at my appointed time. Through my faith, I will be able to bring forth what I have been diligently expecting. I will see the rewards of my labor that God has laid up for me. My faith teaches me to stand up straight. Dig my heels in and refuse to give up on, give in to, or to simply give up and let go.

Faith encourages and engages me (you) even during some of my (your) weakest, darkest, and dire moments. Faith tells me (you) to keep moving because it doesn't matter what it looks like, sounds like, acts like, and feels like. Faith tells me (you) to keep focused on what's ahead of me (you), remembering to continue to press in and press through the visible until I (you) no longer see any remnants of myself (yourself), just the purpose of the Gospel that is being birthed through my (your) faith. Paying no attention to the sound, the noise or the cares or the jeers of this world, God is for me (you) therefore, absolutely nothing else matters or can stand against me (you). Recognizing that I (you are) am victorious in God! I am (you are) an overcomer in God! I am (you are) a winner and God sees me (you) as having already accomplished the goal at hand. Praise ye the Lord!

The actual assurance from faith to me comes from the past experiences and outcomes of what I have person ally witnessed God do in my life and the life of my family, friends, and loved ones. The assurance is the outcome of what I had previously envisioned would come to pass. It is the exact outcome of what God had ordained over 2,000 years ago before for my personal journey, before I ever entered into my mother's wound.

The assurance is God's ability to pull out of me the "yet to come" and place it in my spirit of the "right now" even before it has ever been thought of. I am mindful that God can light a fire directly into my past to begin praying and yearning for a particular blessing, outcome, or longing well before I can dream or imagine its possibilities and or its name even coming into fruition.

This is exactly why the call over and on my life is bigger than gossiping people who don't want to see me enter in what is rightfully mine. It's much bigger than my haters who don't think that I deserve to enter into the realm of breakthroughs and breakouts that God has ordained and set forth for my life.

Despite the injuries, the war zone, the outside and some inside pressures; despite the setbacks, setups, cutthroats, and left outs, I must move forward in order to assist in advancing the Kingdom of God as it relates to the call and mandate on my life. It cost Him too much to die upon the cross for me just so that I can live my life in a dormant, lazy kind of way.

God is more than able to bring about what matters most to me and more importantly, what matters most to Him and His Kingdom building. God is more than able to bring it to pass and cause it to manifest for His glory! Praise Him! I am learning each and every day that the hardest part of the journey is choosing to only believe what thus saith the Lord has already spoken over your life.

~ The Substance That Faith Is Made Of ~

The confidence that what we hope for will actually happen…

In my private study time in the Word of God, my understanding is that in order to wholeheartedly receive what we are hoping for, we must first be able or at least have the ability to perceive the impossible. An individual must be capable of permitting their lives to go beyond the normal activities of their daily routines, schedules, and boundaries to accept that with God, all things are possible. One must first allow themselves permission to dream big, beyond their wildest dreams and limited possibilities. Neither sets nor allows restrictions, borders, hang-ups, and what-ifs to shut down their heart's desire.

Substance to me represents the very fiber, the connection that literally binds and impasses the darts from *hoping to have*. It is that godly ordained connection that God has already set forth in motion and destined for us to finish strong and actually receive tangibly on this earth before the very beginning of time. In other words, if God has already approved of the vision for our lives, we should at least be willing to accept and follow the provisions He gave us to term; after all, He has already paid the cost plus penalty and interest.

I can remember for years going to bed and literally seeing myself ministering before the masses. Waking up rejoicing and praising until my pillow was soaked and wet. Crying out to God for more of Him and less of me, desiring to become more for the Kingdom building and not for the hand claps, the cheers, or approval of mankind. I have lived long enough and experienced enough backlashing to know the cost of that already. Although I did not understand at what price that desire would come or what measure of faith it would take, I still chased after it nonetheless, because it was not about the fame and temporary "glory" that one normally seeks.

Daily I would write in my journal and date the conversations to go back and remind myself of what I was hoping for at that particular moment. I believed that God had fashioned and placed me here on earth for the greater and not the lesser. If He has caused others to walk in their destinies, surely He has not forgotten how to get me to where I needed to be in record time.

For I truly believe that in accordance to Jude 1: 24–25, "now unto him that is able to keep you from falling, and to present you faultless before the presence of his glory with exceeding joy, To the only wise God our Saviour, be glory and majesty, dominion and power, both now and ever. Amen."

That particular scripture would always lift up my spirits because it showed me personally the capabilities and the enormous authority that our God has. Indeed, in His name, there is no lack. No weaknesses. No limits. And no boundaries. When He called us into existence, He looked at us in the exact same manner as being whole and complete, lacking nothing, and announced that within us lies the Greater, which is Himself and that because of our relationship with Him and only through the shed blood of Jesus Christ upon the cross can we be privileged to accomplishing all things through Him which strengthens us.

Notice the scripture says, "Now unto him that is able to keep you from falling…" I believe the scripture was not necessarily talking about not ever making a human mistake or taking an incorrect turn here or there, but rather, one would not utterly be cast down forever, that our lives or circumstances would not literally circumvent the will of God for our individual lives. But that God would use those very circumstances to take us higher than we have ever been before and use those life lessons learned as a stepping-stone to arrive at the necessary point or pivotal moments in our lives.

The word *faultless* to me in this term does not speak of *perfection* but rather because the blood of Jesus has already been shed for our lives over 2,000 years ago back on Calvary. It is really finished, and no one or no circumstance, issue, problem, or critic can hold our faults, mistakes, mishaps, issues, or misfortunes against us again because God's Son, Jesus Christ, has already paid it all! Praise God! None of us has to worry or concern ourselves with the views, opinions, thoughts, criticisms, hatred, malice, and the lies of others because none of that has any real value in what they think about us anyway.

Only God is able to present us *faultless* because He alone paid the ultimate price. The only price applicable, and when He said through His son that it was finished, He meant it was finished! Done, complete and overruled! The matter was over with and never to return; so now when I personally encounter mean-spirited, evil, unkind words that come from the mouths of individuals who I know do not have a real connection or relationship with me, I con-sider the source or sources from which it came and tell it, "Excuse me, that's not my mail, please return to sender!"

The Word of God continues to say that not only is God the only one able to present us faultless and to keep us from falling, but He alone can and will do so with *"with exceeding joy."* Hallelujah. Only our God can do that. Why? Because God is the only wise God, the One who knew us before, during, and after this life on earth is over. He fashioned each and every one of us and called us His beloved! That in itself should be enough validation to last a human a lifetime.

I don't know about anyone else, but it doesn't get any better than when our Heavenly Father validates us. After all, who can override His verdict? He is the judge, jury, spectator, and the outcome of it all. God is the only one who has the authority and right to do so; and it is at His commandment, without the input or suggestions of others.

Whereas mankind is very quick to jump to conclusions and assume the worst in others, God sees it differently, and thankfully, He is very slow to anger. Man only dotes on the outside of another, but truly God is the only one who really knows the outcome of it all. He does not see us as "the fallen" but rather as *the redeemed* of the Lord! When God looks down for any one of us who has been redeemed through the blood of Jesus, He doesn't even see the individual, but His Son who was crucified upon the cross in our stead.

In the words of Pastor Joseph Prince, *"God sees you in Christ. When He sees you, He sees the cross, and through the cross you look beautiful."* After all, it is about the cross and not about the person per se and their self-righteousness.

It took me years and years to accept the fact that the true approval and validation that I really needed was that of my Lord and Savior Jesus Christ. I am almost embarrassed to think about literally years and years of my life I spent trying to appease and gain the approval of others that I looked up to and actually respected. Only to realize that for some of these individuals, had I known what I now know, they really didn't deserve or warranted either in that moment.

It was often very disconcerting to befriend others who rejected me or didn't see or treasure the value that I brought to the table. It was difficult, at best, to listen to them speak only about my flaws and weaknesses that they deemed were important, at least in their natural eyes. I now fully under-stand that God is more than able to handle all of my flaws, weaknesses, imperfections, and misfortunes, and turn them all around for my good.

I can remember being in the presence of certain individuals who would comment on the negative things about me and never point out the positive attributes that had visibly been accomplished or that I was striving toward. For example, when I gained weight, there were those individuals that were quick to say, "Oh my goodness, you have sure gained a lot of weight." "Look how big you have gotten." As a good friend of mine, who shall remain nameless, often says, "Oh really, why state the obvious."

As soon as they got the knee-jerk reaction that they were probably hoping and praying would result from their insult, they were only too quick to ask, "What's wrong, are you okay?" Because I didn't know then what I now know for sure, I would too often allow their small minds and even smaller comments to practically ruin my day while trying to figure out why anyone would willingly make such curt and derogatory comments.

However, today, being delivered from all that is evil, what I know for sure is that "if God be for me, who can be against me?" In other words, their thoughts, actions, words, criticism, support or the lack thereof, is to no avail to me, because at the end of the day, I really can do bad all by myself. However, knowing that God is for me and that He loves me is all the validation that I need or desire. I no longer need, look for, or even wait for the consent, appreciation, validation, and support of others to propel me to move forward because what I now know for sure is that God is all that I truly need. He alone is my refuge, strength, and source. I can stand still and wait for God to place those in my life where we can be an encourager one to the other.

Until I was able to finally break through the bondage and the real hypercritic mannerism of it all, I was never fully able to live my life freely and without fear of being talked about, limited, judged, mishandled, misunderstood, labeled, and iced out of the "sister-circle and at the tea and crumpets meetings—I'm sorry, I meant to say ministries, so to speak.

What really matters most now is that I am free from mankind's bondage, judgments, legalism, religiosity, church-folk mentality, rituals and stigmatisms that only apply when they are applied and imposed by those who deem themselves as being temporarily in control. I don't know about anyone else, but I am gladly sticking with the One that paid it all for me in Calvary, the One who keeps me daily!

When I think about having the confidence of the things that I hope for will actually happen, that takes self-confidence to believe in my God-given talent, skills, craft, and ability that has all been provided through His might to accomplish the things that He began in me.

Confidence to me means being assured, having the assuredness, poise, and the coolness to deal with everyday pressures, stresses, and issues that come along, especially once my mind is made up to move forward regardless. I consider myself to be a living testimony that when you decide to move forward, there will be some who will walk out of your life, reject you in some way, and probably delete you from their phone's contact lists. There will be others who may deem that the climb is too steep to follow suit or that the risk is too great, and therefore they will leave you jilted, abandoned, and sometimes deserted if you allow that one moment to define you.

The confidence that what we hope for will actually happen

What is extremely important to know is that where there is pressure and rejection, I promise you, if you'll just decide to move forward and stay focused on the Lord, victory is often right around the corner. When pressure comes, it is usually to try our determination, test our limits and find out our boundaries. Remember, if God is for us, who can be against us?

Sadly enough, there will be those who enjoy seeing the pain inflicted from rejection or the cold shoulder given to another. They run with tumultuous speed to spread the news of doom and gloom concerning the downfall of another. They often enjoy seeing the dejection, misery, gloom, unhappiness, and sadness of others who they feel are less fortunate, less educated, or undeserving than themselves.

They appear to get a thrill from the sheer thought of others struggling and dying for the love and acceptance of those they hold so dear. Yet when the same method or measure of fate is dealt to them, many find themselves, drowning their sorrow in pills, medications, drugs, lies, deceit, backstabbing, or other self-destructive measures trying to deal with life as they know it.

I want to encourage anyone today who may be reading my book to not allow others' scare tactics or intimidation to humiliate you to the point of turning back from what you believe God has called and fashioned you to do. Run if you must run, alone. Walk, crawl, or hitchhike; but whatever you do, never, ever give up on you. Choose to believe that your God is enough validation for you. Remember, indeed, the race is not given to the strong but to the one *"who will hold out and endure until the end!"* (Emphasis mine)

> *I returned and saw under the sun that…The race is not to the swift, Nor the battle to the strong, Nor bread to the wise, Nor riches to men of understanding…(Eccles. 9:11)*

Most people in the world today would confess that they probably would be farther ahead in their personal goals and journeys if they had the support, love, and genuine happiness of those they cared very deeply for. The truth of the matter is that there are those who are so afraid to think out of the box for themselves without the fear of facing ridicule, judgment, peer pressure, envy, strife, and, sad to say, even hatred from those they may hold in high esteem. It is very unlikely they will ever have the courage to move forward.

Fear and rejection has a genuine way of causing us to run back to the very thing that causes us so much pain, stunts our daily growth, and temporarily shuts us down. I remember a specific time in my life when I allowed others to decide how I would dress, wear my hair, sometimes critique me on what my interests were and how important they were to me based upon their suggestions and very cloudy judgments about how they perceived me to be. I mean, I knew better than to put too much trust and/or confidence in others, but during some of those days, I really didn't use my voice to stand up for myself as much as I should have.

Looking back on some of those moments, I realize now how ridiculous those years were; but sadly enough, I gave away my power. I temporarily allowed the enemy to steal, borrow, rent, lease, and, yes, steal my God-given identity and what He had fashioned me to be. God did not create me to become a robot or a doormat for anyone. I was never created to be a yes person, and if that meant walking alone until the right friend, spouse, career, opportunities, or tea party came alone, oh well.

Thankfully, today, I can honestly say that I am not that same little girl, teenager, young adult, or grown woman any longer. Today, I am capable, fortunate, and very much aware of who I am and whose I am in Christ. I am persuaded and wholeheartedly convinced that according to Romans 8:38–39 (KJV):

> *For I am persuaded, that neither death, nor life, nor angels, nor principalities, nor powers, nor things present, nor things to come, Nor height, nor depth, nor any other creature, shall be able to separate us from the love of God, which is in Christ Jesus our Lord.*

Today I know for myself that God is good. He is my refuge and strength. He is my strong tower and mountain mover. My source and my resource. He is my comforter and confidante, my buckler and my shield, but more importantly, He is pro-Brenda, and that makes me smile, and it gives me an exceptional peace and an undisturbed assurance that all is well beyond human measure or capability.

I no longer look for signs, wonders, and ten people to touch and agree with me. I no longer feel or have the urge to walk around things seven times until I get dizzy trying to remember how many times I went around the building before I needed to stop! In fact, I no longer need others to necessarily believe in my dreams and ambitions before I believe that God has caused me to dream bigger dreams and imagine things that I once deemed were totally out of my grasp, because I was too afraid to dream big.

Even though, admittedly, I cannot stand Lucifer, I cannot really blame him for all my fears and phobias because I realize now what I didn't know can and will often stunt my growth. What I didn't know caused me to walk in doubt sometimes, second-guessing myself. I relied upon the "advice" and often-inconsistent responses of others who weren't necessarily always in tune with what God had for me, and perhaps hoping that I would never find out. This caused me to miss out on things that were relevant for my growth.

However, today, I have truly been delivered from major strongholds that fought me over the years to comply and simply just give in to and not press on for the greater good for my life. The strongholds tried desperately to get me to become settled and content where I was. They wanted me to submit, and sometimes just omit the call on my life altogether. They challenged me to just become ordinary and blend in with everyone else's mindset on living.

Even when I attempted to advance, whether it was through my education, ministry, or just in my sheer happiness, I was challenged because what I did not know then that I know now was that opposition can be viewed as an opportunity to advance further if I was willing to move ahead despite the rejection by others or the hurt I felt as a result thereof. I now know and understand that I am never defined by hindrances or obstacles, but rather, I can choose to allow those things to catapult me into my next level of advancement simply by choosing to forge ahead.

~ *The Evidence of Faith* ~

*Now faith is the substance of things hoped for,
the evidence of things not seen.
—Hebrews 11:1*

    For me, the evidence is the possession of what I've waited for, hoped for, prayed for, and even longed for, that would be my expected end. The evidence means the support or the source that I am relying upon to bring what is expected to a visible, tangible, and fruitful end. Evidence comes after the labor, the work, the discipline, and sometimes the experience of the thing most desired.

    Evidence is birthed out of your heartfelt knowing. Your gut-wrenching desire to prove to yourself that something is possible despite the challenges, circumstances, and disappointments that may lie ahead. Evidence means the search for more and better is plausible, which means that some-thing is valid, apparent, acceptable, and even warranted.

    The fact of the matter is, through Jesus Christ, the price for our sins—*all* have already been paid; therefore, we have no earthly reason not to move ahead in Him, because there should be no condemnation from others that will cause us to walk about the earth with our heads down as if we are still in sin debt, because we know and have been taught through the Word of God that our sins have been forgiven by the Almighty God!

We now know that through Him, we have been redeemed. In Him we live, move, and we already have our being. The truth of the matter is we are overcomers—the head and not the tail. We are above and not beneath; the lender and not the borrower, the whole and the healed of Him, resisting all sicknesses and diseases, lacking nothing. You may ask me how I can boldly say this—it is because of all the evidence that points back to the same place—the Cross! Evidence to me, that shows me free and clear, evidence that means that every victory in His death emphasizes a new creature being empowered to get out of jail and be free in Christ to move in the plan and purpose for my life!

Not only are we free in Christ, but we are free to move about on earth as He alone has fashioned us to do so. Through Him, we can move about with confidence, assurances, joy, love, peace, and longsuffering with others. We no longer have to ask Satan for permission to be happy, whole, delivered, or joyous. We can move about the earth with a teachable spirit, humble posture, and not with a pious attitude, as if Jesus died for only one person.

The Word of God proclaims, "Go make disciples," not to become caught up in the tangled web of who is qualified to reach and/or teach the disciples once we get to the designated place where the people are. All who are called of Christ have this mandate issued to them to go make disciples (Matt. 28:19). I believe it is to cause men and women's hearts to change whereas before they only lived unto themselves, but now having come into the knowledge, wisdom, and understanding that Jesus Christ paid it all, they are compelled to live their lives as a living testament so that others will know that there is someone Greater than themselves.

I believe that the world at large, major entirely too much on the minor, on the unimportant things in life, often overlooking what really matters most—the souls that are at stake who don't know Christ but would like to. We should strive to live our lives daily so that others can see glimpses of Christ displayed in us throughout the course of the day. It should be our daily quest to live so that everyone will see the difference between the two (the old man and the new man that has been born again).

According to Bing Dictionary, the word evidence means information, deposition, and affidavit. It also means evidence, exhibit, testimony, proof referring to information furnished in a legal, investigation to support a contention. I wonder today how many Christians are sending mixed messages according to how their lives are being lived out in the privacy of their homes; their work ethics, and to the general public.

Are we being mindful that it doesn't matter whether we know anyone is watching us or not, we must be careful to allow the light of Jesus Christ to always flow through us? Daily, we must be eager to decrease so that He can increase and forever reign as Lord over our lives, Monday through Saturday, so that Sunday-morning worshipping or church-going is just a formality because we have the evidence of Christ living inside of us.

~ The Value of Experiencing Faith ~

The value of experiencing faith is when you know that you know that whatever God has spoken over your life is already yes and amen!

The value of what I call experiencing faith is experiencing for yourself that God really loves you and that He cares unconditionally about you. Although He has the whole world in His hands, you are one of the most valued, beloved creations of all time, and we are constantly on His mind.

God does not have you confused with anyone else. He really knows your name. Your identity is hidden in Him alone. Your purpose, your desires, your DNA is in His will. God does have a blessing with your specific name on it, and no one can change that or alter His specific purpose and will for your life.

The value of that knowledge and understanding is priceless. When you fully grasp that concept, it is mind-boggling, to say the least. It dispels any lie from the enemy. In fact, it stops him cold in his tracks because not only does he realize that God has spoken, but that you have in fact heard Him and agree with His verdict over your life. The very last thing that the devil wants a child of God to do is to believe God and take Him at his word; not only does this upset the devil, but I believe that it makes him literally nauseated, to say the least.

There is nothing more freeing than to know that we are His beloved and that He loves us without any hidden agenda, strings attached, or hoops for us to jump through. His love is actually unconditional. It does not matter if we are up or down, He loves us. Rich or poor, He loves us. Misunderstood or mishandled, He loves us. Whether we tell the truth or lie, He loves us, and He only wants the very best for us.

When something is valued, it is held in the highest esteem. It's considered priceless to the holder or the recipient. It is appreciated, respected, treasured, cherished, and prized. To a born-again believer who has placed their lives in the hands of the Lord, they have come to experience the love of the Father, and nothing can penetrate that realm because they understand that it does not get any better than this.

Faith releases one to dream big. To stretch out in God and set their face like flint until they receive what it is they are personally hoping for. They are not quitters in the wake of issues, trails, tribulations, hardships, and challenges. They understand that the only way through something is the willingness to travail and tunnel through to the other side. Their trust squarely lies in the hands and at the helm of the one who said that He alone was, and is, able to do all things but fail.

The value of that personal victory in Christ can, and will, never be forgotten, especially when you reminisce and remember the numerous times He has delivered on His word and never, ever broken a promise or brought you out of every little, bitsy, tiny incident.

The real value in experiencing faith is not taking the word of others, who at times may try to talk you out of your deliverance, victory, blessings, and breakthroughs, because they just don't understand your plight at the moment or the specifics that God is working in you and through you. They don't fully understand how you can possibly be smiling when you have just lost your child, your marriage, your home, your job, or your health.

Sometimes outside folks try to strain to see how it is possible for another individual to maintain their relation-ship with Christ after having been through hell and back. They've heard about your sicknesses. They've heard about your failed career, they witnessed one negative result after the other, and they are still amazed at the effort you make to keep moving forward, despite it all. They don't fully understand that you will not quit until the battle is over.

Even in their curiosity, and oftentimes dismay, they would rather guess than believe that your God is more than enough as the evidence points to day in and day out to keep you in what may appear to be a tragedy or a life-threatening ordeal.

The value of experiencing faith teaches the believer how to hold their heads up while travailing THROUGH the temporary trials of life and not giving in to your emotions while doing so. Often, when people are going through a certain situation, they look worried, stressed, challenged, or bothered. Not looking this way does not necessarily mean that everything is totally all right; it just means that you have some concerns that need to be worked through.

Their minds are often filled with thoughts relating to their particular situation. They try to figure out how they are going to come through it, or if they are somehow ever going to come through it; and what happens if they don't come through it? Not allowing themselves time to realize that God already has it all in control before anything ever took place or the weapon had even formed.

I have learned so much during my and my husband's last ordeal that even while being in the midst of it all, we are not what our circumstances and personal situations look like. Upon closer examination of the thing, what we were being delivered from daily was the shell casing of what was left of our problem as God was making us anew. God had, in fact, used the very thing that came to destroy us or bind us at the appointed time of deliverance, to lose its hold and grip and set what it thought was the captive free indeed.

Knowing, believing, declaring, and decreeing that our God is more than enough to handle any and every problem or situation that will enter into our paths was enough for my husband and me. Daily, we acknowledged the Lord as being our refuge and need meter over every single problem that we faced whether it was naturally or spiritually speaking. There wasn't a day that went by that I didn't recognize how the Lord sent to us the appropriate help that we needed. Daily, we were aware of how He allowed us to literally stretch out in God and to remain at peace during the journey. I fully embrace the fact that the Jehovah that I rest in declares that He will go ahead of me and make my crooked ways plain. That He will fight every battle for me if I just keep still. I am certain that God personally oversees the dynamics of it all. Absolutely nothing escapes Him. He is in the personal details and fibers of our daily lives.

In fact, my husband and I have personally learned how to endure the storms and become suited up spiritually speaking, before, during, and even after those particular storms are over. One day while we were talking, my husband said to me, "You know, babe, most people feel that being on the mountaintop is what is important because everyone can see them; however, I've found that being in the valley is more vital because mountaintop experiences are usually short-lived, and the valley teaches you how to be sustained during the duration."

So the real value of experiencing faith is knowing for yourself that all is well, even before the outcome is revealed. It's having the right belief about the God that you believe in, and that He alone has the capability, power, credibility, reputation, and ability to bring you out, no matter how dire or seemingly impossible the situation and circumstances appear to be.

The value of knowing Jesus Christ as Lord and Savior of our lives is absolutely priceless; the mere fact that Jesus Christ is the King of Kings, the Ruler and Maker of the Heavens and the Earth; and the ending and the beginning of it all, and that He still desires to have fellowship with mankind is breathtaking.

Experiencing God for real is a tangible and reliable resource that will last forever. Because it is a knowing that cannot be taken away from you. Experience in and of itself is a life lesson instructor that comes alone to teach us that during these pivotal moments in Christ, we can trust Him and take Him at His word. Without experience we will not know if He is able or not. We will not know if He will deliver us or not. At some point, we have to take the extra step and decide to move forward.

Growing up, I remember vividly asking God question after question about the plans He had for my life. Not understanding and not having the inner ability to comprehend the vastness of it all, I wanted to know everything right then and there. Weekly, if not daily, I would find myself pleading with God to show me the plans He had for my life. I just wanted to know and thought with all sincerity that I could readily handle what those plans were.

Shockingly enough, I now realize that had He shown me perhaps a glimpse of what I have experienced and walked out thus far, I would have surely toppled over right then and there, and for certain, I am confident in saying that I would not have made it through the first challenge!

Trust and rely on the fact that God is not only a God of order but also one of timing. He knew that it was not just about showing me His plans for my life but, rather, about building me, growing me, training me, preparing me, and fortifying me for the plans in my life to come. God is about sustaining us. He knew what it would take for me to grow. He knew that the temperatures of some of the furnaces had to be just right in order to shape my life to the level it is today.

He knew that through life's various experiences, whether they were perceived by me as being good, bad, or indifferent was not so that I would have the opportunity to pick and choose which of the ones I would rather have, but that they would bring me into direct alignment with His per-missive will for the grander purpose of it all.

He knew that the entire scope of my life was for the express will of Kingdom building and so that others would be able to see His good works through my living out loud the plans that He executed through me. God's purpose for my life had very little to do with me being pleased or approving of the plans, but rather, it had more to do with me being able and willing to trust Him and the willing-ness to weather the storm during the plans whether or not I could see Him performing the miracle, sense Him being close by, or discern Him in the details.

God never brings His children to a door without the ability of taking us through it. I am a living witness; some-times He removes the hinges, sometimes He leaves the specific door(s) open, sometimes He deliberately shuts them; or sometimes He just simply brings you around it altogether. It doesn't matter; one thing I know for sure is that He will deliver you, and He will do so on time.

It is my honest belief that God is far more interested in preparing me for Kingdom building and leading or pointing others to Christ than making sure that my flesh is glorified in daily rituals or worldly positions that might point others to me instead of Him so as to appear more important than I really am.

~The Feedom of Laying It All on the Alter~

I appeal to you therefore, brothers,
by the mercies of God, to present your bodies as a
living sacrifice, holy and acceptable to God, which
is your spiritual worship.
—Romans 12:1 (ESV)

It is said that altars were places where the divine and human worlds interacted. Altars were places of exchange and communication, and where influence took place. I believe that the altar is a place where one can go privately to display his or her true gratitude and thankfulness unto the Lord for what they have received. It is a sacred time, a blessed and hallowed time, rendered unto God that is normally shared by the two. No one else needs to know, accept, or, for that matter, understand the purpose of the time shared at the altar other than the two. Being able to meet God at the altar, a place of gathering that could be as simple as a specific room in your home, in your office, your car, at church, or what have you, the type of altar is not as important as the meeting itself. God just wants to have us alone, with Him, so that we can have that one-on-

one fellowship together without interruptions.

Having that unadulterated freedom and liberty to do so is vital and extremely liberating. To know that one can talk with God about any and everything, where nothing is off the table, out of order, too big or too small; whether it is unimportant or plain dumb, God delights in hearing from his children. He wants to be a part of every facet of our daily walk.

He is concerned about what concerns us. It is important to note that our God already knows about us. Every thought, every issue, concern, and circumstance. He does not need for us to necessarily tell Him anything. However, He delights in our sharing and coming together to commune with Him about our concerns and to share our hearts with Him.

I believe that God wants to fix and handle everything that concerns you and me. He is more than able to do exceedingly and abundantly more than we can ask or imagine. According to the King James Bible, Ephesians 3:20, "Now unto him that is able to do exceeding abundantly above all that we ask or think, according to the power that worketh in us," God is more than willing and able to take care of our every need.

The freedom to come boldly before the throne without condemnation, hypocrisy, shame, judgment, embarrassment, degradation, trepidation, or the fear of hearing your private thoughts or comments being told throughout the land is refreshing in itself. God is a God of order and integrity. Praise the Lord!

I, for one, am so very grateful that God is not like man. For starters, when entering into the presence of the Almighty God, you can rest assured that He already knows all, yet He still wants to have divine fellowship and dialogue with me. He already knows my end from my beginning; yet He still wants to hear my voice and my concerns and my desires. Just the thought that God wants to know my intimate thoughts, fears, worries, and concerns makes me glad.

He delights in calming all of my fears. He specializes in my aches, pains, hurts, wounds, mishaps, mess-ups, and slip-ups. He knows how to speak to a racing heart, sooth sweaty palms, divert nervous reactions and unexplained and untamed anger management and out-of-control tension. God knows it all. Yet He still sends me an invitation to come boldly and confidentially.

I can trust that He will keep what I have to say in the utmost confidence and will not sell me out. He will not

think my desires and dreams to be impossible or too small, unimportant, childish, too big, or irrelevant. God really cares about the details of our very lives. Not only does He care, but He wants to be instrumental in every minute detail of our daily walk. In fact, His word declares,

> *All things have been handed over to Me by My Father; and no one knows the Son except the Father; and no one knows the Father except the Son, and anyone to whom the Son chooses to reveal Him. Come to Me, all who labor and are heavy-laden, and I will give you rest. Take My yoke upon you and learn from Me, for I am gentle and lowly in heart, and you will find rest for your souls… (Matt. 11:27–29, ESV)*

While in the midst of my personal storms, I have discovered that I could not have been in better hands. In fact, I would venture to say, being in the eye of the storm is what probably truly saved my life and gave me true meaning for a more meaningful life.

Being in the storm that God allows you to enter into gives you permission to rest, wait, hope, delight, trust, and see the storm for what it is. Storms, to me, now come into my life for specific reasons and purposes. I now view storms in this manner:

S = Staying close to the Master's side
T = Trusting that He will see me through

O = Operating in the wisdom from on high
R = Resting in His capable arms
M = Moving forward despite what it looks like
S = Scheduled to arrive on time

When one is invited to bring it all to the altar, it is not just an ordinary plain old invite to stroll down memory lane with a few items in tow. I realize that bringing my all to the altar affords me the opportunity to truly fellowship with the One who knows me intimately and much better than, I dare say, I know myself.

Literally being able to converse with the One who knows me intimately is priceless, because it takes the guesswork out of knowing my place in the universe. Or trying profusely to verbalize what I cannot readily visualize. Not only does God have a plan for my life, but He is eager to share those plans with whoever is interested in knowing what they are about.

Laying your all on the altar is about being transparent, exposed, naked, unashamed, plain, not hidden, released, forthright, and obvious with your Maker. It is coming forward without condemnation or any hidden agendas. It is also about fellowship; open unaltered fellowship; and truthfulness. Additionally, it's about acceptance of who you were created to be without excuses or apologies.

Being able to approach the altar with realness and truth is a gigantic step toward true healing, understanding, forgiveness, receiving, taking personal ownership, being authentic, and being one-on-one with the One who knows all about me. When I come to Him, I can come boldly, with a full disclosure that my entrance into His presence is not about my brother or my sister's faults or shortcomings. It's about me being able to stand in the presence of my Lord and Savior and share my heart.

It's enough just to be able to know that I do not have to rehash my sins from years ago or bring Him up to date about my past, my mistakes, my hang-ups, my failures, or my private pain. God is more interested in relationship and fellowship than anything else. I believe that He wants me to know that He loves me through my good and my bad. And that once I am in His will, absolutely nothing can separate me from His love.

We should view the invitation of the approached to the altar as being about you and God. Everyone else and everything is excluded in the moment. Absolutely nothing else matters in that time frame or specific space but truth; and that's God's truth, not our recollection of what we think that truth represents. Because sometimes in our own human efforts, we may define truth as being what we condemn as our explanations into why we operate the way we do, or why we responded the way we did, or why we react in the manner we do.

The altar experience is a very sacred moment that can be spent very meaningful if we will open up and possess the willingness to receive from God. We must be willing to hear, receive, and accept truth from God and execute the purpose that He has for our lives. We must never discount or count out what we call the "little unimportant" things that God views as necessary and vital in our lives for our daily progress and growth.

We must not view approaching the altar as a moment of being scolded or a time of condemnation but, rather, as an opportunity of growth, expansion, and expectation. A level of excitement about what God has to say to us that will change our lives forever.

I now view the altar as a place of true release and fulfillment. It is an enchanted moment with the one I truly love and, more importantly, that really loves me and accepts me for what and who He created me to be. Since embracing this mind-set, I have never felt more liberated and free in my entire life. In this moment, I am experiencing no limits or boundaries because my mind is set on Christ or my mind-set is centered on Christ and His thoughts toward me.

The altar is also a sacred place of shedding whatever binds and holds you down. It is a place of experiencing pure freedom and liberty firsthand. At the altar, there is no one there to stand in judgment of you or your deeds. There is no one there to cast the first stone. There are no viable accusers waiting to pounce on you and to accuse you of your wrong-doing or thinking. The only one standing at that altar with you that really matters most is your Lord and Savior, and He is not there to condemn you or to criticize you.

In fact, the Word of God declares in John 3:16–18,

For God so loved the world, that He gave His only begotten Son, that whoever believes in Him shall not perish, but have eternal life; For God did not send the Son into the world to judge the world, but that the world might be saved through Him. He who believes in Him is not judged; he who does not believe has been judged already, because he has not believed in the name of the only begotten Son of God.

That should be excellent and exciting news to all believers, as well as nonbelievers. We have more than a chance to make it into the kingdom of God; we have a golden opportunity to do so at will. God has made it affordable through the payment of the shedding of His Son's blood to enter in freely. The altar is about intimacy with your Maker. It's private, personal, intimate, sacred, and nonintrusive. It's a chance meeting with the Creator of the Universe at will.

~The Validity of Things Not Seen~

Faith is believing in something greater than yourself when everything within you tells you to run the other way and don't look back.

According to Bing, validity in science and statistics, is the extent to which a concept conclusion or measurement is well-founded and corresponds accurately to the real world.

Raw faith to me is being able to stand firm on what I know, to stand firm in what I have personally experienced and have received from God. It is choosing to trust in God without a shadow of a doubt as it relates to my personal relationship with Him. The validity of my tangible relationship with God is something that gets easier day by day and can be shown to the world and those around me simply through my living. No matter how much scripture I believe I know or how well I know how to pray, it is nothing like trusting in God for my everything, because on many levels, it is a reaction that cannot be ignored—perhaps not always easy to explain and/or understand, but it is readily noticeable.

Let me explain as best I can. My husband had a stroke in September 2012, just shortly after Labor Day. We are, and were, a family of two that always did just about everything together. When you saw one, you saw the other. We have always had each other's back. We care very deeply for each other.

So one can only imagine my arrival at home one Thursday evening after work and finding my beloved husband on the floor of our office in the midst of having what the doctor's described as a "severe or massive stroke." This took my breath away and scared me to no end. The first and only name that I can remember calling was Jesus!

For the next two years, this incident not only changed the normal dynamics and normal flow of our household, it also propelled the both of us, in some ways, in our different journeys to contend with, both good and evil in our personal and spiritual lives.

While my spouse became a patient, I became the immediate sole provider (earthly speaking) for my household, the caretaker of my spouse, and the overseer for all of our household affairs. Immediately, I found myself being thrust into a totally different and necessary role. This, after all, was real time and not some horrific dream from which I was scheduled to awake anytime soon.

It was now our reality, for who knows for how long. To say this was very scary would be a gross understatement. It would test the very fabric of my belief in God, not in what I had already experienced in God, but moving for-ward. Looking back, I knew Him for years as my savior, my keeper, my strong tower; however, things were now unraveling right before my eyes at such a rapid pace that I didn't have time to remember all of His names referenced in the Bible. I just had to rely upon Him as being Lord of all.

Almost immediately, once various folks (family and otherwise) found out, conclusions began to be drawn and were blasted across the board; almost everyone had their own opinions, input, and thoughts about how I should tread from that point on. I understood that many did not know my life or our lives from the outside looking in, and still I chose to believe that their intentions were perhaps for our good, no matter how far-fetched at times they seemed to be.

Sadly, most people could not look beyond what they believed to be the obvious solution, and that was to automatically downsize from our standard of living and move in a different direction altogether, as quickly as possible. Not even being familiar with my circumstances or, necessarily, my situation. What most failed to realize was that years prior, seven years to be exact, the Lord spoke to my heart and said in no uncertain terms, I have a house for you. He shared the details from the foundation to its end. Seven years later, we moved in, and that is where we remain until this day.

Still, there were those who asked me repeatedly, what in the world was I going to do? What was going to happen to my spouse? Were we still living in our same home? Driving the same cars? Able to work? Did I even have a job? I mean, just what was I going to do? What was the plan? As you know, to the world, everything is about a plan. Even if the plan has no vision, just have a plan! Even if the plan has no virtue, structure, or substance, child, just have a plan.

Hearing those barrages of questions one right after the other automatically instructed and equipped me with what I knew I needed to do—become yielded, focused, stead-fast, and unremoved by the world's care, especially when they were sometimes asking from afar with no intentions of assistance. I knew how to pray and did so daily; however, this time I was more relentless and gratefully driven. Daily, I continued to pray. To rely on, depend on, and totally trust God, all in that order.

To some degree, from the outside looking in and not being armed with any real truth from what was really happening, I suppose I could kind of understand where they may have been coming from. Sometimes when one is standing on their front porch and watching a storm cloud move in, suddenly without being forewarned, not only can it be a bit overwhelming, but sometimes there is no time to take cover.

From my point of view, God allowed me to pray specifically four nights before the storm originally started to brew; so when it actually materialized, He was the shelter that steadied my being. In the storm, the more I quieted my spirit before the Almighty God, the more He ordered my steps in specific rhythm with His will and purpose for my life. One day I heard Him say to my spirit, If you serve my servant, I will take care of you.

After all, fear has a way of causing people to regard things differently in a given moment. It's kind of like looking at a blueprint that is not quite developed yet and trying to detect what is the next move or step without any insight from the architect.

I realized that perhaps from our family's perspective, I chose to believe that they may have been coming from a place of concern and genuine consideration. After all, when others are outside of the scope of another person's life and lifestyle, the first thing that takes place is assumptions, perceptions, and their interpretations of how they see things. It doesn't matter if they have any knowledge, revelation, or forethought about whether or not it is remotely the truth or not, just that they might possibly have an opinion that might work.

In that moment, I must admit that I made it my personal business to not fall prey to any negative comments, gossip, heresy, rhetoric, idle talking, or just straight- out lies. I knew that other's opinions about us, whether true or false in that particular moment did not add any validity, truth, or real benefit to our current situation; and I could not afford to adhere to the negative realm.

I realized more than ever that the first real thing that I needed to do in our new journey was to dismantle everything that was not godly ordered or ordained. It didn't matter where or who it came from.

At that moment, I didn't need or appreciate anyone trying to quote scriptures that they themselves were not living by or unwilling to uphold. I was unwilling to listen to stories or comments about how someone else had gone through similar experiences, but the end wasn't good. I immediately shut down and carved out every negative thought that rose up against us in the name of Jesus.

My immediate stance was to position myself in the Word of God, where I could hear solely from Him alone. At that time, what I needed was direction, clarity, peace, compassion, and definitely wisdom from on high, and nothing else would do.

Suffice to say that during this time I was met with curt words, hostile spirits, arrogant individuals both working in professional settings and otherwise. I crossed paths with more people telling me what I could not do than there were people lifting me up.

Without a doubt, there were those who blatantly told me outright that my spouse would never get better and that I might as well face the facts. After enduring countless months of being berated by hospital professionals, nurse advocates, and rehabilitation facilities, I decided I was not going to back down. I was not going to waver in my approach to the Almighty throne. I was going to stand and make my daily request known unto Him who sits on the throne, no matter what.

The amazing thing about grace, I found out in that hour, was that grace is a person, and His name is Jesus. And once the enemy threw his best punch and did everything imaginable to us, he was then upset because we still would not bow or give in and quit. He could not understand why we were both still entertaining the thought of victory on either side.

He could not understand why we were relentless in our desire to continue to praise God even when the world thought that we had already gone through so much, and now this? Surely they must have done something wrong. Mistreated someone, and now this is their punishment, right?

People really started talking when at the time of my spouse's illness, our household went from two well-paying incomes to me working two part-time jobs. On my first job, I earned a paycheck every other week; and from the second job, I was paid once a month.

And to the world, it looked foolish that I would even think that we could survive on either…but God!

The validity of things not seen, revealed to me that truly in order for my family to not only survive but in order to thrive, we together had to enlarge our thinking capacity and regulate our spiritual mindset on what or who we were meditating on constantly. We already knew that not only was it not about us in that moment, it had never, in fact, been about us.

We knew and fully understood that the Word of God in Isaiah 26:3 declared, "Thou wilt keep him in perfect peace, whose mind is stayed on thee: because he trusteth in thee." And at the moment, we were more desperate for His perfect peace than trying to make nice with our enemies or to appease those who had no real stake in our outcome, one way or the other.

It was imperative for me to get a handle on just who was in charge of my life in that regard. Was it going to be my emotions, my feelings, my status or the lack thereof, the world, my coworkers, family, friends, or my haters?

In that moment, the only real thing that mattered most was whose report we were really going to believe about our lives. It was a no-brainer to see the obvious; however, to decide to stand still and see victory took grit. It took stamina and declared staying power in Jesus. Was it easy? Absolutely not, but then again, no real victory ever is.

Within the first month, when I was challenged the most, I had actually spent the night in ICU with my husband, and I had watched him have a seizure, swelling on the brain, and another mini-stroke in less than one hour. The news was becoming more and more grim, and according to the doctor's, it was not in his favor; however, once again, but God!

The next morning as I was on my way home from the hospital, I chose to not listen to the radio, CD player, or even pray. I drove home in silence. I asked God to show me what to do. I needed to hear clear concise details for my situation. It was at that time that I heard in my spirit this message: "And I make my sheep to lie down in 'green' pastures." While I was familiar with Psalms 23, I knew where it was coming from, in this particular context. I wasn't absolutely sure of what God wanted me to glean from that thought, so I inquired of Him.

Upon further questioning and listening, He explained to me that He has a way of hiding his sheep under His shadow and to preserve them in what man may consider some of the most slippery, unimaginable, unsafe moments, where even his closest enemies cannot find them, even in the tightest surroundings.

It does not matter how many, how large the crowd may be, how long the tunnel has been dug—the trap has been set, the lies have been told, the roadblocks put in place, and God is still able to turn it around to your favor.

Month 1, God instructs me to be at rest in His presence. To seek Him first and foremost (don't look to my left or to my right), that He alone had everything in control. This was September, and we had already been working on a conference that had been scheduled two months before my husband's stroke. Now in addition to taking care of him and working two jobs, maintaining the household affairs, fighting with opposition, and maintaining my sanity, I still had a conference to oversee.

It would be one Saturday morning after leaving the hospital that the enemy really began to taunt me. He said, "Really, are you even remotely thinking about having this conference when it's just you left? You have all this to con-tend with. No one is coming to support you, why don't you just cancel the whole thing and try again."

All the way home from the hospital that morning, he continued to taunt me; and for some strange reason, that morning, I chose to listen to every word that came out of his mouth. Not only did I listen, but I chose to listen fervently. By the time that I arrived home, I had reached my conclusion, and that was "Thank you, Mr. Satan, you have truly blessed me this day. I was almost considering cancelling the conference, but I remembered asking God for confirmation about what I should do, and you just gave me all the legitimate reasons why I should. You are absolutely correct in stating the obvious that I cannot do this alone especially in and of myself, but with God, all things are possible. Oh, I failed to mention to you that the title of the conference was 'Courage Under Fire!'"

As for the scripture reading:

"When you pass through the waters, I will be with you; and when you pass through the rivers, they will not sweep over you. When you walk through the fire, you will not be burned; the flames will not set you ablaze. (Isa. 43:2, NIV)

Not only was this conference necessary, but it was a topic and scripture reference that God had given to us in the month of January of that same year, months before we ever thought this would be happening.

In my mind, that was confirmation enough. I chose in that instance, to simply move forward. Scared and nervous, I decided to look unto the One who was more than able to do exceedingly, abundantly, more than I could ask or imagine.

Not only did the conference go on without a hitch, but the people who attended were blessed. It wasn't until after the conference was over that someone whispered to the other about the possibility of my husband being admitted to ICU just a couple of days prior.

When questioned while in the process of leaving the building if it were so or not, I replied yes, but I still had to move forward with the work at hand. Little did I know that in that moment, the women from the conference had decided on the spot to take up a special love offering that took care of the entire conference cost, but God!

Trust that God will not demand that you readily "see the thing out in front of your naked eyes that you are hoping for," because that is not what true faith is really all about. If you can see it, you don't need the belief or trust factor in that moment because it is already tangible right before your eyes.

Faith is receiving the tangible news or "spiritual expectation" or exhortation in your being, or knowing about a concept, thing, or outcome prior to the outset of what you are deliberately waiting or hoping for.

Here's an example: Prior to my husband and I moving to the current house we now share together, it would be seven years prior that I had received a word of exhortation from the Lord that He was preparing and giving me a home. Not only did that word of knowledge come to me directly, but the specifics and details of how that was going to come about were given to me as well.

So as I fast-forward from that moment to now becoming the sole breadwinner and overseer of my home, I could stand on the promises of God because He had already given me insight and made me privileged to the knowledge of how to respond in this or any other situation concerning our well-being.

So when this trial of testing came, I didn't have to second-guess myself or our situation because God had already given me and my spouse what I call the withstanding power to do so. It didn't matter if others understood, gave approval, agreed, or provided their independent blessing—God Almighty had already done so, and we believed His report.

Because those around me were not privileged to this understanding, some automatically jumped to major conclusions about what direction I should take. Quick, sell your home, downsize in your entire way of thinking altogether. After all, there is no way you can still afford to remain living the way you are now, they said.

Not once stopping to perhaps realize that maybe, just maybe, God was at the helm of it all. That perhaps in that moment, what my household may have needed most was encouragement, support, love and a little genuineness. It is so important for others to realize that in the time of crisis, the last thing that one needs is criticism or someone else's opinion or evaluation of how well they are doing.

I decided I was not moving to the left because I was utterly assured of what the Lord had spoken to me years prior. Needless to say, in every hardship, trial, testing, jab, or undermining, the enemy came at us, trying to break us and hinder our personal walk with the Lord; by choosing to stand on the promises of God, I witnessed God doing more than provide victory. He also provided steadfast-ness as well. He stayed me and my family at every level. Therefore, we grew stronger in our faith and our dependency upon Him. We didn't just survive—we thrived daily, in relentless victory.

Daily, we expected God to provide. He not only pro-vided, He would show up and super-exceed our very existence in His coveted Will. He provided, and then some. It was not always about monetary means that we were blessed; He also provided for us supernaturally in wisdom and confidence, that He went before us and made all of our crooked paths plain.

There would be times when I would try to transport my husband from doctor's appointments to other appointments, and I would be struggling to get him into the car because he wasn't able to provide any assistance at all. It was also very challenging to get the wheelchair both out and into the car, as well as get him out of the car and into the doctor's office and so forth.

At that time, my spouse was not able to speak as freely and relied upon me to be his voice and caretaker all the way. The majority of the time, when we met for appointments, one of the first things that the doctor's would ask was, "Are you his guardian, and do you have his power of attorney to speak on his behalf?"

One of my memorable times of getting my spouse to one of his doctor's appointments is when we were leaving the Veterans Administration Office. It was raining outside and extremely cold. I wheeled Audie to the outside doors and placed a blanket over him as I ran to the car to bring it closer to the door. As I struggled to get his chair close to the car, it was very difficult to get him up and out of the chair, making it virtually impossible to get him into the car. We both were getting soaked and wet in the cold-icy rain.

After six or seven failed attempts to get him into the car, I looked around for possible help. In doing so, there was this very large front window with these two very obvious, well-abled young men just standing their gazing out at us struggling. As soon as they realized I noticed them, they quickly dropped their heads and turned their backs to the window and never looked up again.

In that moment, I realized I only had one option, and that was to keep my focus on the matter at hand, which was praying and asking God for direction and to please send immediate help. Looking into my husband's eyes, I could see the helplessness because he knew that he was unable to help me help him. It crushed him to think that I had no help from anyone to assist me with him. Suddenly, he lowered his head and closed his eyes.

It was in that very moment, I felt my Redeemer airlift me as though I was suddenly thrust upon and strapped into the seat of a Boeing 727 Jet. Supernatural strength came suddenly and as I turned around to look again into this building, there was a woman now staring out at us and something within me told me to leave Audie propped up besides the car and go back into the building now!

Knowing the voice of the Holy Spirit, I didn't even hesitate. I covered him from the cold and rain and went back into the building. Soon after entering the building, I asked the woman staring at us, did they have any security guard(s) that could assist me? In a very unprofessional tone, she said, "No, we don't have any guards or anyone that can assist you like that." And then she turned and walked away.

Within seconds, this very tall, mature gentleman pushing a wheelchair in my direction overheard our conversation and looked me in the eyes and said, "Ma'am, just a minute, how may I help you?" I told him I needed assistance getting my husband into the car. He said, "Let's go," and we both went outside into the rain and cold, and I watched him struggle with all his might to assist me. I could tell with every lift of sacrifice of assisting Audie into the car caused him pain; nevertheless, he never stopped trying until he was successful.

After thanking the gentleman, I got into the car and drove away, tears running down my cheek. I simply raised my hands in total praise and adoration and whispered, "Lord, I trust you!" Just then, I felt a sense of peace wash over me as if to say, Be still and just know. And when there was no tangible help and hand made available, we could depend upon God to send a word of encouragement through a stranger's prayer on site. Words of encouragement and kindness. Indeed our God is an awesome God, and He alone reigns forevermore.

The validity of enduring our daily walk in this vein taught me that I had nothing to fear because God was going before us daily and making our crooked paths plain. He was exceeding our limited expectations and showing Himself strong from all aspects. The validity of my faith, in that hour was the confidence I readily experience in God at every level and turn. Even in my incredible noticeable weakness, I could say without ridicule, embarrassment, hindrance, or babble that God was, and continues to this day to be, our one constant help in all things.

There were times during this testing that I was stretched so thin and challenged so severely (in the temporary storms) that I clung to God for dear life. I would pray, "Lord, I believe that today something great and miraculous was going to happen to me and my family, today, tomorrow, and the rest of the week." Daily, I would not allow my feet to touch the floor without saying, "Go before me Lord and make all the crooked paths plain." Each day, without fail, I could trust God to direct my every step and move. Whereas there were people that I turned to for earthly strength, it was important to me to know and fully understand just who they were.

Note to self: I learned very quickly not ever to identify my storm with someone who does not have my best interest at heart. Because by doing so, I might be better off weathering the storm alone, rather than inviting others to watch me drown or, at the very least, go under while in the temporary battle of the storm. One thing for sure is that while there are some who may not be able to stop or pre-vent the storms from occurring in your life—at least they will be able to offer an umbrella of coverage while others will sometimes just leave you out in the cold.

However, the validity of faith to me is refusing to be moved, unnerved, agitated, irritated, sensitive, shaken, stressed, or to lose your immediate focus while you are in a temporary situation, even when you don't understand it, like it, or that you can move around it. The validity of my storm was not about how I felt about my temporary situation or if I could fix the situation or not—it was more about how I was going to allow God to get His rightful glory in my situation.

I understood one thing, and that was, like it or not, even though the storms were rough and terrible, the Almighty God was working it out for my good; and no matter what we may think about storms, when I held on to the fact that it would be nobody but God to deliver me and my family to the safety of the shorelines, I dug my heels in, steadied my faith, and decided to finish strong.

I knew that there was absolutely nothing that I could do on my own. I could not control the circumstances or the fact that these things were happening to and around my home, health, finances, or our lives; but I did know some-one who could control the storms and their temperament at all times. The least I could do was respect and obey the One that could.

Many times, in the moment of despair or being overwhelmed, it would have been so easy to throw up my hands and just die a slow antagonizing public death. But instead of doing so, I remembered that God allowed me to be placed on the front line of this battle, not to be demolished, depleted, defeated, or to become demoralized by my circumstances; but He placed me there to stand still and see the salvation and get the victory that is rightfully due His name.

Validity to me is about proving the authenticity of something being tested to see if the thing before me is real or not. One of my jobs, I believe, was to test the trials that were positioning themselves before me to see if they were what they represented themselves to be in the wake of my faith. However, what the test and trials didn't know was that each time they knocked at my door, I never answered in my own strength and might because I already knew that I could not handle them, so I allowed the God of my faith to do so each and every time, and there was not a moment in our journey that I didn't push the envelope of our faith, love, relationship, and overall ability to thrive in Christ.

Against all odds, we chose to stand firm in our conviction that Jesus was Lord. No matter how many countless late night and early morning hospital trips, no matter how many negative hospital reports, no matter how lean and tight things got, we chose to rest in the arms of the Almighty God and believe that the Lord was our Shepherd and that we shall not want for nothing. My reply was, "At least we are not stuck. And anytime you are mobile that means you are continuously moving."

Someone may ask how you could do that when you have been through so much. My daily prayer was, "Dear God whatever you do with us, please do not allow us to come to a screeching halt where there is no continuous flow of your presence, power, or provisions in our lives." Indeed, the Lord was a constant stay. We knew that the Word of God states in Jeremiah 29:12–13,

> *Then you will call upon me and come and pray to Me, and I will listen to you. You will seek Me and find Me when you search for Me with all your heart.*

A lot of times, I encountered questions such as: Isn't it hard to take care of your spouse by yourself? How are you managing with everything? You know you can't do it all by yourself now. You must stop and take care of yourself or learn how to ask others for help. Really, wow! Thanks for the brilliant idea. It wasn't that I was totally oblivious to any or all of these things. I knew that it would do me no good to be lead astray by my emotions or feelings. Rather, I must rely on my wisdom, discernment, and understanding.

Seriously, I suppose from the outside looking partially through the window of someone else's house, it may appear that the answers are just that—cut-and-dried or issued out to you in a cookie-cutter fashion. Not! Often when life hits you with unimaginable, unpronounced, deliberate, and sometimes debilitating circumstances there isn't a plan already in place. You are not going to be able to reason, cry, naturally fight, and or explain your way out of it because sometimes, life just readily happens.

Sometimes, it will take some travailing. Sometimes it will take some lamenting unto the Lord; it will take courage under fire. Trusting God unconditionally while persistently being pursued by your enemies or the trial at hand, you will never know the true power, magnitude, or fortitude of a present Help by the All-Knowing God over your life unless you are willing to go through and endure some things as a good solider.

That doesn't mean that you won't get weak, tired, over-whelmed, discouraged, and maybe even a little disillusioned along the way, but you must remember, He is a very present Help in the time of trouble. "Trouble" in the Greek means He's the God in our "tight places." We must learn how to refuse to worry; instead, we should look up so that we can move up.

Just when the sunshine appeared to be peeking out from under the makeshift clouds, life had another curveball for me and my family, this time in the form of cancer. Yes, in January of 2014, I started feeling very tired. Not just men-tally, but physically speaking. I noticed during the day, and most often at the end of the day, that I was totally drained. All I wanted to do was just simply lie down and rest.

Oftentimes, by the time I reached my bed and laid down, I was out like a light in a deep sleep. There would be times when someone either called or came by the house, and I never heard a thing. They would tell me later, "Girl, I came by." Or, "I called you, and I couldn't get in touch with you. Are you all right?"

Usually my response was, "Yeah, I was just tired," and left it at that. For some reason, I started thinking about how much I needed a serious vacation and how badly I needed time just to myself. Over time, this thought became a daily desire that I processed hourly. By the time February rolled around, I was making my request known to God that I desperately needed this time away. I didn't want to have to concern myself with any details regarding anything. I was tired and needed a rest period.

Daily, my request would be, "Dear God, please hide me behind a mountain where no one would know me, some place where I would be able to rest and regain my strength. Some place where I can just find shelter in your arms." I wasn't interested in outside fellowship. Lunch dates, reading books, I just wanted uninterrupted rest and to hear only His voice minister to me.

~ *The Expected End* ~

"One of my very private and personal prayers to God has always been, "Lord, even if I lose my material things that you have given to me. Even if my marriage should suddenly end in divorce or even if the ministry no longer existed, the one real and tangible thing in my life that I will always long and hunger for is your great grace, love, and mercy in my life.
I cannot ever lose my hope in You, for You alone is all I will ever need!"

By March, I honestly could not think of anything else more important than my time away from everything and everyone. I wasn't angry, I wasn't upset. I just wanted to steal away and be alone with my thoughts and God.

Little did I know that I would soon be doing just that in a roundabout manner. One night, while sitting up in my bed eating cookies, a couple of crumbs fell and rolled down my chest. In an effort to remove them, I gently brushed the crumbs away, and I felt a lump in my right breast; and immediately, a soft but ever-so-present voice said to me in my spirit, Cancer. Determined to not receive the news, I dismissed it and looked the other way.

A few minutes later, the voice encouraged me to re-exam my findings. Nervously, against my entire rationale, I did so. To my surprise, there it was again—the hard, seemingly visible lump in my right breast. Streams of hot tears liter-ally rolled down my checks. I covered my mouth so that I would not scream out loud and awaken my spouse who was sleeping ever so peacefully beside me, totally oblivious to what his wife's new findings were.

In that moment, I threw back the covers and headed for the nearest bathroom and continued to cry, this time looking in the mirror. Hand still covering my mouth, I whispered his name, Jesus, as if He was physically standing right next to me in the room. I reminded myself in that instance that God was able, in my now-desperate and what-appeared-to-be-isolated moment. God was able!

As my mind was spent racing about what seemed to be 10,000 miles per minute, I held on to grace and mercy for all it was worth. I didn't plead the blood of Jesus because I knew if He had, in fact, brought me to this moment, surely he had already meted out the journey before me, and I knew His promise was to me that He would never leave me or forsake me. I continued to cry, being fully persuaded that tears was a language that God fully understood. So that night, I decided to go back to bed. Wrapped myself up in His word and hold fast to what I knew: He was, and is, my healer.

Still, on Sunday morning, I said nothing to my spouse about the "supposed" lump I had found in my right breast. I went about my day as if it was just an ordinary day, hoping that my previous findings were inaccurate and in error. During the whole time, I knew in my heart of hearts, I was 100 percent accurate.

Psalm 40:31 (KJV)—"But they wait upon the Lord shall renew their strength; they shall mount up with wings as eagles; they shall run, and not be weary; and they shall walk and not faint"—became my mantra. Literally, I know that if I had a 1 percent chance or remaining sane, I needed to draw closer to God than I had ever been in my entire life. There would be no room for wavering, doubting, or complaining. Trusting God explicitly and holding fast to my faith was all that I chose to focus on.

On that following Monday morning, while getting dressed for work, I took a deep breath and decided to check again, and true enough, it was still there. This time, I chose to accept my reality and move forward. Having already made my annual mammogram appointment, I put the matter aside and decided to move forward with our annual spring women's conference, which is always held in March, usually around my birthday.

During this year's annual conference, I decided on the title "Unrestricted Praise." I realized that no matter what was happening in my life, I needed to still continue to send up the praise because God did not have to allow me to find the lump in the first place and spare my life up until now. I realized that in that very moment that the God that I trusted was definitely up to something big in my life.

I decided to notify my entire family myself and tell them of my discovery. I started with my beloved spouse first, and of course, it was extremely difficult for him to hear, but we leaned on each other. Declared and decreed, we chose to believe that God was on our side above all else. As for the rest of my family, they took it all in as best they could, at least on the phone with me; how they responded afterward, only God really knows, but they put their best foot forward at the outset.

I chose to tell my family early on, because I didn't want them to be in the dark or have any fear(s) that God would bring me through this and that we would be just fine even while "going through" the shadow of death, because the Word of God promised to be with me and us along the way. I trusted Him with all of my being.

The next couple of weeks seemed like a dream, at best. The conference went well, and even though it was a lot of work, I looked forward to its debut. What I noticed more than anything was how tired I was in the process. I would be so tired that all I really wanted to do was just sleep. Every chance I got, I slept and slept. Even though I considered myself to be a light sleeper, during this process, I would end up in very deep sleep patterns and would still be tired when I woke up.

So I began to pray for a vacation of about six weeks specifically. I just wanted time alone with God only. During this time, I only wanted to hear His voice, feel His presence, and consider His Word over my life. Daily that was my request, "Draw me nearer to you, Lord. Nothing else would do." I found myself thirsting after Him with a voracious appetite. Day and night, I sought Him, knowing that He would already be present. I found solace in just saying His name.

Finally, the day came for my mammogram appointment on March 31. I went and requested additional testing because I knew that this would be no ordinary mammographic exam. The woman was curious as to why I was requesting additional testing. I explained to her my findings, and she still thought that I didn't need to go that far. Knowing better, I insisted that the extra testing be done and I was not leaving until it was.

Reluctantly, she took the extra precaution but was still visibly upset because I insisted that it be done. As I was getting dressed to leave, I was approached by another nurse with a great big smile, who asked me if she could please talk with me for a moment after I got dressed, in her office. I said yes, and afterward, we went into her office and sat at her desk. There, this quiet-demeanor nurse very candidly stated, "Now, while no one wants to hear the word cancer, your testing today could quite frankly return with that result, and I want to assure you that if that is so, it will be the facts; however, we know that God's Word is truth, and it over rides everything else."

My mouth literally dropped open as I stared at her. She talked with me as if she had already gotten the test results back. She smiled and held my hand and asked if she could have a word of prayer with me before I left for the day. Still shocked, I said yes, took her hands, closed my eyes, and we prayed.

Her voice and her demeanor were extremely soothing. There was something about her demeanor that spoke a sense of peace over my situation. She explained to me that she herself had gone down this same road and that God had healed her body and that what He had in fact done for one, He could and would do for me.

I left that place that day feeling very thankful and hum-bled by the entire experience. In the following weeks, I expected a letter to arrive notifying me of their findings. Sure enough, within weeks, the letter did come, with the confirmation that it was cancer. Thankfully, I knew that the Almighty God had already gone before me and made every crooked way plain.

The letter provided specific instructions about what I was supposed to do in the following days, which were to get approval from my primary doctor to come back in to have a scheduled biopsy and an ultrasound before moving forward. I called and scheduled my annual doctor's appointment with my primary doctor and went to see her.

While she was examining me, I told her about my findings in my right breast. She said, "Oh, it's probably just fibroids, nothing to really worry about. I'll check them out to see, but I wouldn't start worrying just yet." She was scolding me due to the fact that my blood pressure was 190/70 and there was a large cyst on my ovaries. She wanted to have me admitted that day. But God! She was so angry with me that she sat down and screamed "Where have you been, and how could you allow this to go on for so long? Don't you understand how dangerous this is? Your health is at risk. Where have you been?"

Not fully grasping how or why I could be this calm, she asked, "Do you know how much trouble you are in right now?" I began to share with her my journey. I told her that the reasons that I could remain calm in her office was that I know beyond a shadow of a doubt that God had ultimately kept me in the midst of it all. I shared with her about Audie and my journey through his sickness. How many near-death experiences he had had within the last six months. Instead of the hired help assisting me, they robbed, stole, and squandered things that were rightfully ours, how they essentially had taken these things behind my back.

I told her that for the past year and a half, my beloved husband had suffered a massive stroke and had been hospitalized from September 2012 to December 2012. That when he was released from the hospital and we were able to go home, the hospital, nursing homes, rehabilitations had fought me with everything they could to drop him off in a facility, because I would not, according to them, be unable to take care of him, because as you know, I only worked two part-time jobs, and I did not have the "necessary skills" to take care of him.

I continued to tell her the reason I could remain calm was probably because I was busy working the two part-time jobs, trying to make ends meet. Running an entire household, dealing with doctors, nurse advocates, battling insurance companies, debt collectors, shysters, liars, haters, crooks, schemers, and just daily critics in general, and when I found time between it all, I rested in the arms of Jesus.

The reason I wasn't angry, upset, distraught, bewildered, or downtrodden about my situation now was because I could look back on my Savior's track record and see that I could trust Him with my life, and that it had been Him alone who has been the very One who kept me, steadied me, and watched over me every single day. In fact, in the process, He whispered to me, "If you will serve the servant, I will take care of your every need." Ain't God all right?

So the mere fact that I had gone through my day and had not fainted, stroked out, had a major heart attack, or all of the above was, simply put, just God! I explained to her that while in the midst of it all, He kept me from all alarm! She just simply stared at me and didn't make another sound. She signed the paperwork for me to fax over for my second opinion at the mammogram place and said good luck.

On April 10, 2014, I went back to have my biopsy and ultrasound performed, and nothing prepared me for the excruciating pain I would have to endure. I wouldn't wish to inflict that kind of pain on my worst enemy. As if having the biopsy wasn't enough, afterward, there were two additional mammograms performed while my breast was still in total shock and in a lot of pain.

Directly after the biopsy and the bleeding ensued, this same woman whom I had spoken to just days prior came rushing back into my room and proceeded to help me. Calling my name while I was still lying on the table, she reached her hand out to me and squeezed it, saying, "Now, Brenda, remember what we previously talked about. I don't want you to be unaware that the results of this biopsy today could very well result in being cancer. However, that would be a fact, but we know that God has the final say on it."

After I was dressed, we went back to her office to talk some more, and she informed me that she would person-ally monitor my results and get back with me immediately following the findings. I could tell that she was genuinely sincere and involved with my exams. I thanked her and left for home.

The weather was bitterly cold that day, and the pain was unbearable. As tears ran down my face, I cried unto God, "Lord, please go before me and make all the crooked paths plain." I cannot explain it other than to say I never took my eyes off of God. He alone was my counselor, my wisdom, and my discernment. I knew all along that I was in good hands. I didn't want any of this to be true; however, I knew that I had to tunnel through this storm because it was assigned to my destiny. The good news about this storm was that it was being monitored by the best meteorologist in the world. I learned that every storm has an expiration timeframe prior to its final destination.

After returning back home, still in pain, I placed an ice-pack on my breast, took two Tylenols and tried to rest as best I could. By now, my husband was crying and saying, "Baby, please don't leave me. I need you. Hurting and all, I looked at the sincerity on his face, and my soul melted from his personal pain and anguish. I saw pure love and fear in his eyes, all at the same time.

Pain and all, I threw back the covers and walked over to his bed and held him close to me like never before. At first, we allowed our tears to flow, and we just hugged each other tightly and accepted the facts. After about fifteen minutes, we both got a Kleenex and shifted into second gear and said, "Now let's review what's before us."

I said to my spouse, "Your illness was called a massive stroke, and now mine is called cancer. Let's agree to not give one more power, right, authority, ability , or control than they deserve to have. Last I checked, there are two scenarios that come to mind. The first one goes like this: 'But he was wounded for our transgressions, he was bruised for our iniquities: the chastisement of our peace was upon him; and with his stripes we are healed' from Isaiah 53:5. The second one is Philippians 2:9–11. 'Wherefore God also hath highly exalted him, and given him a name which is above every name: That at the name of Jesus every knee should bow, of things in heaven, and things in earth, and things under the earth; And that every tongue should confess that Jesus Christ is Lord, to the glory of God the father.'"

I reiterated to my husband that "since both of our issues have a name, let's agree to submit them both under the name of Jesus, and since the Word of God has just confirmed that "Wherefore God also hath highly exalted him, and given him a name which is above every name: That at the name of Jesus every knee should bow, of things in heaven and things under the earth."

Beloved, there is a name which is above every name, of things in heaven and things on earth. That name is a name to which every knee must bow, and a name that takes precedence over sickness, pain, relational failures, addictions, lack of any kind, depression and despair, and yes, dear ones, even hopelessness. This name is Jesus.

Jesus is the Son of God.

This Jesus was the Son of God, who came to earth in the form of a man, but He went to the cross and was crucified for you and for me that we might become the righteousness of God through Him. He could have called down legions of angels to deliver Him from this ultimate sacrifice, but because of His great love for us, He suffered the crucifixion. And now through His life, death, and resurrection we can proclaim (declare and broadcast) that by His stripes we are healed and we have been reconciled to God.

It only seemed befitting and appropriate that this would be a good time for the both of us to cast every care, stronghold, concern, matter of interest, stressed-related burden, or anything that concerned us under His feet and His name. We believed that in the name of Jesus, every knee should bow, of things in heaven and things under the earth. That day, we held hands, and with one voice we cried out, "Massive stroke and cancer, in the Name of Jesus, you have now been cast under the feet of the Almighty Jesus and the blood of the Lamb who has already been slain on our behalf." After doing so, we never went back to retrieve it since.

On Tuesday morning, I was still in pain but understood that my husband still required my assistance in every way, so I prayed silently and asked God to make it easy for me to assist him, and He did. As I was preparing for the day, the Holy Spirit reminded me that I needed to go have some blood work done at the local clinic, and I did so.

However, on the way back home, I stopped and bought us breakfast and walking across what I call the "cat walk" at our home, I literally heard in my spirit, I am the Lord thy God who healeth thee. In that instance, I knew His voice, and I threw up my hands and immediately went into a praise and worship segment—just me and Jesus.

That was my confirmation that it was true, it was cancer; but God had gone before me and had indeed made my crooked paths plain. It was exactly four hours later when my phone rang from the hospital with the same familiar nurse calling to inform me that they had the results back and that they were, in fact, positive that the diagnosis was cancer. A moment of silence followed.

The nurse asked me, "Brenda, are you there?" To which I replied, "Yes, I am." She said, "Okay, let's move forward." She appeared to have a vested interest in my well-being. She said, "Looking at your film and other tests, I can see the cancer appears to be the size of a pinto bean, sitting in a strategic place in your right breast area. It's funny, though, because if I didn't know any better, it's as if someone simply placed it there for us to readily find it."

She continued to use specific phrases and wording like, "appear to be," "as if someone did," "watching over you and guiding you." She went on to say, "The lump is placed directly behind the nipple of your right breast. It almost seemed as though if I could lean you over far enough and hit you in your back, and it would simply fall out onto the floor. Someone indeed loves you very much."

The lump had not metastasized. It was not even a stage yet. It was between a centimeter and a gram and did not appear to be aggressive in its growth. But God! She said, "Our next move from here is to get you in to see a doctor right away and to provide you with the very best we have on staff. The doctors are all at lunch right now, but just as soon as they return, we will get you scheduled for the next step."

Within thirty minutes, the nurse called me back with great news. "I have you scheduled for Wednesday afternoon to meet with a doctor, and from there, you will have other necessary appointments scheduled throughout the rest of this week. My niece was kind enough to come over and drive me to the doctor's office. We arrived on time and met with the doctor, who was extremely sweet.

I continued to cry out to God, and He instructed me quite clearly that before I attended the already-scheduled doctor visits, I was to attend them with pen and pad. Take specific notes and listen. Do not enter into agreement with anyone. Do not sign any paperwork that would enter me into a contract with anyone. And ask only pertinent questions.

When we walked into the room, the first thing after the introductions the doctor turned to me and said, "Brenda, I just had to meet you personally because you in your profile and you in the flesh are two entirely different people. The actual trauma done to your body does not match the woman that I am speaking to right now. Tell me about her."

I told her about what the last two years had been like for me, lifting my husband in and out of bed, shouldering all of his weight on my body frame, taking him to doctor's appointments, and getting him in and out of the car, twice a day. About working two part-time jobs, running a household, going to work and coming back home on my lunch break, making him lunch, returning to work and working extra hours to make up for the hours that I missed to take care of him, just to name a few…

Tears rolled down her face. She said, "How did you do that?"

"But God" was the only response that I needed to say, because it was, and has, and will continue to be all God! There wasn't a dry eye in the room that day. We continued to talk, and she laid out her plan for me, with the options. Even though she said we could have the surgery by next week on Tuesday, something within me said, "Wait." I knew it was the voice of God, and so I did.

Before I left her office, she carefully wrote down our entire office visit conversation and provided me with the correct language in which to share with the other doctors I would be meeting with going forward. She even provided me with the results of the x-rays and mammogram that I had previously taken. I left her office feeling encouraged.

From that day forward, there were those that knew of my temporary situation that continued to ask, "What are you going to do? What are your plans?" To which I would always reply, "All is well." I knew instantly that in order for me and my household to survive this test, it would only be a test that God had allowed me to take, but that the answers had already been supplied, and I knew that He had deemed me able in His might to pass.

The next several doctor visits would prove to be interesting, to say the least. The reconstructive doctor made the entire visit more about him than it was ever about me. Actually, from the time I drove up and entered the building, I sensed that this place was never about his patients but, rather, more about his personal accomplishments. His walls were outlined with his many, many accolades and trophies; there was absolutely nothing about the caring of his patients.

Several days before going to see him, I went on their website and completed the application so as to speed up my visiting time. I even called to confirm that they had received the application and any other pertinent information needed.

I was trying desperately to preserve any vacation, sick, and/or medical time that I had remaining for when the time came for my surgery. Every day I would declare and decree, "Lord, I thank you that you go before me and make all my crooked ways plain. Heal me O Lord and I shall be healed; save me and I shall be saved for You alone is my praise" (Jer. 17:14)—that was my mantra for the journey, with no exceptions!

Upon arriving at this particular doctor's office, it didn't matter that I had completed the entire application online weeks beforehand and called to ask what else could I do to assist their office with my impending visit. They took their sweet time and never once showed any concern for me. I was told to wait in the lobby until someone came for me. I literally waited for the doctor one and a half hours before the first sign of any human interest.

When the doctor did show up, he showed me a listing of previous breast reductions, surgeries, and implants that he had performed. Need I say he was quite proud of "his" work. Not once did he inquire of me the purpose of me being there, or had I given any thought as to which direction I wanted to go. Even when I offered some input, I was over talked by him and his greatly inflated ego.

At the end of the visit, he was quite annoyed by any questions and/or concerns that I appeared to have. His every response was, "I am a doctor. You have to ask my assistant those concerns. I have performed surgeries like this for over 23 years. I think that I know what I am doing." What he failed to understand was that my concerns weren't merely about how many surgeries he had performed on others; I was concerned at the moment about myself.

I was concerned with the difference between a lumpectomy and full blown mastectomy, of which he did not want to answer, and quite frankly never did. In fact, he offered me a pamphlet and said "Call my nurse and make an appointment when you decide." Before leaving, he informed me that if I was leaning towards mastectomy, I should move forward with a "double mastectomy" because it would only be matter of time before I would be having both. After all, this is what he does for a living.

Once again, I prayed, "Lord, I thank you that You alone have gone before me and made all of my crooked paths straight." I decided to set my face like flint and kept it moving. The next office visit would be to the oncologist. One thing for sure that all the doctor's visits had in common was that no matter what, they were going to get the co-pay first and foremost, no matter if you were entering heaven or had a few minutes to spare in preparation for the journey home. Their only immediate question was "Do you have the $40 co-pay?"

By this time, a coworker had committed her time to go with me to each of my doctor's visits because she had gone down this road herself and was encouragingly aware of how it all worked. She was my rock in those hours of moving forward and for that, I will be forever grateful.

Once the paperwork was completed at the front desk, I saw the nurses and waited for the next step; however, there appeared to be not another step planned. We basically just looked at each other until I began to ask specific questions. I was offered a snack while I waited and everything else appeared to be just normal activity. When I inquired about the protocol for a lumpectomy, once again, the subject matter seemed to shift immediately.

The nurse took a deep breath and immediately changed her attitude. She asked, "Well, what do you want to know?"

My reply was, "Well, everything there is."

She really offered no answers, just a series of additional tests and a brand-new biopsy without any type of anesthesia. I said, "Absolutely no way." I am human, not an animal. My body is not built to take raw pain.

The nurse said, "Well, we can give you a prescription for Xanax."

"No, thank you," I replied. Instantly, I knew that this was not the place for me, and that I was never coming back there. Eventually, I paid my co-pay, and we left.

My next appointment scheduled for the next day was with the radiologist. I decided to cancel because I had not decided upon the actual date for the surgery yet, and therefore the radiologist appointment could wait. Once I got outside of the building, almost to my car, out of nowhere, a different nurse came running out, hands waving in the air, screaming, "Come back, come back, did you just cancel your last appointment with the radiologist?"

I said, "Yes, I've changed my mind about coming tomorrow." Not only was she shocked, but she was extremely rude in the process.

She said, "What? Wait a minute, when did you decide this, and who told you that you can do this? You are going to need radiation and chemo, no questions asked."

By this time, enough was more than enough. I turned to her and asked, "Who decided that, because without even looking at my records, talking with me, or my previous doctor, how could you have come to such an abrupt conclusion on your own?"

Looking like a deer that had suddenly crashed through her own headlights, she could only say, "Well, that's how it normally goes."

My reply was, "Thank God I am not an ordinary, normal person. The word of God tells me that I am uniquely made into his expressed image, and besides, I walk by faith and not by sight. Your 'norm' is neither my reality nor my destiny" and proceeded to my car and drove away.

From that time forward, I never had another doctor's appointment with anyone in Texas. In fact, I continued fasting and seeking the face of God, as I had been doing with the other ladies through our daily conference calls from 6:00 p.m. until 7:00 p.m. The next week went by, and after talking with other family members, my big brother agreed to come to Texas and stay with us while I had my surgery. I was so grateful and will always be in his debt for that act of kindness and love.

During the last week of fasting, my niece, Ruby and her spouse stopped by the house to assist us with a couple of projects, and she asked me, had I ever heard of Cancer Treatment Centers of America? I told her yes—however, I never thought to contact them in this process. During our conversation, in that moment, I decided to call them, and a nice gentleman answered at first, and then passed me along to a nurse advocate.

I will never forget her name: Karen. Little did I know, she would become the forerunner for my life in the healing process of my personal journey. From the moment that I spoke with Karen, everything about my journey became upgraded in an instance. She was kind, professional, compassionate, warm, engaging, knowledgeable and more than willing to listen. The instant I heard her voice, I knew without a doubt that I had literally heard the voice of God through our conversation. He was there!

Karen knew what to ask. She knew how to assist me. She was confident in her work and her skill set. She never once wavered, and she was present, in the moment with me. She was my earthly forerunner for one of the most challenging fights of my entire life. The more we talked that day, the more it felt like having a personal conversation with a close friend. I felt comfortable, safe, and encouraged to share.

Karen was my mediator. She walked me through the process. She continued to mentor, coach, and check on me almost daily. She became more than a nurse advocate to me. She was that still, calm voice that kept me focused and on track daily.

Before I even entered the property in Tulsa, I received calls and made contact with various staff members from their facility. I was most impressed. I spoke with Karen on Sunday afternoon, sent the release papers on Monday morning, completed the paperwork by Wednesday, approval for time off from my job by Thursday and was ready to go on Sunday.

My sister, Dorothy, from Detroit, met me in Tulsa on Sunday night, May 4, and we moved forward aggressively from there. God was already ahead of us. Upon my arrival Sunday night at the airport, I was greeted by a chauffeur and taken to the facility. When I entered the premises, the other passengers and I were greeted with warm smiles and outstretched hands. I looked to my left, and there was my beautiful, patient, and loving sister sitting right there waiting for me with an infectious smile and outstretched arms. All I could say in that moment was "Lord, how I thank you that you alone are Almighty!"

And it didn't stop there. We were taken to our rooms and checked in, but not before praising God some more before we retired for the night. Monday morning, we hit the floor thanking God and then headed downstairs for the first meeting of the day. In the excitement of it all, I had overlooked what day it was until the Holy Spirit suddenly reminded me that it was the ninth day in which He had previously instructed me that He would show me where I was supposed to be on that day for the steps in terms of my treatments.

When I looked around, there I was sitting in the lobby of the Cancer Treatment Center waiting to see the doctors. Praise God, I knew instantly I was on the right road. Not because of where I was sitting necessarily, but because of who had spiritually brought me there—Jesus Christ and His angels.

Shortly after 8:00 a.m., my name was called, and I was greeted by a beautiful, soft-spoken woman with believer all over her face. She introduced herself as Char and welcomed my sister and me back to the first doctor's appointment. What was interesting to me was that before I even had an opportunity to enter into proper dialogue with the doctor, he entered the room, smiled, and said to me, "Brenda, do you know that your thyroids are enlarged?"

I found that particularly interesting, because I had just visited with my primary doctor, who had made a similar statement, but never attempted to follow up with me for a prescription of any kind. Yet I continued to feel my strength weakening as if I were running out of energy. I could continue to do my work set before me; however, now it would require more effort than previously used.

Now that the doctor had my total attention, I commented, "I do." He smiled and asked, "What did your doctor say about this?"

I said, "Well, she addressed it, but no follow-up was ever advised or mentioned." With that, he said, "No worries, we will get that taken care of today for you."

He was extremely positive, compassionate, and kind. He treated me as a whole person and not just someone who had a "condition" of some sort. I felt totally comfortable with him and knew that God was definitely leading the way and that my steps were being ordered even then.

We moved forward to the next doctor's appointment. I had the same type of experience: no one was afraid to talk about Jesus. No one pretended that they alone had any or all of the answers. They very boldly expressed their dependence upon the Almighty God, and when they didn't express it verbally, they walked it out through their performance.

They handled me as though they knew I was a part of the royal priesthood. One of the King's kids, they encouraged, motivated, and to some degree shouldered some of the care that went along with each step of faith. God is indeed good. After a period of doctor visits, we had a break for lunch, and during this time, we had an opportunity to fellowship with others and to hear about their personal journeys along the way.

For some of the people that we met, you could see hope in their eyes; and in the eyes of others, you could only see fear and doubt; but in the midst of it all, what I know for sure is that when we don't see a way, or have any earthly idea how we are going to make it through a situation, we must hold on to the fact that our God is still in control of everything and He is ultimately the one who decides our every footstep in this life.

After lunch, we were right back on schedule for the remainder of the day. As my sister and I waited in the corridors of the hall, we kept hearing the various nurse advocates and volunteers walk by and say my name, look at their notes and/or schedule, and say something like, "She's ahead of schedule." After a couple of times repeating this phrase, my sister seemingly a little uneasy, said, "What are they talking about?"

I leaned over to her and said, "Don't worry, that's just the Lord going before me and making all of my crooked paths straight." Even while transitioning through this temporary storm, I felt my faith being amped up to another level in Jesus's mighty name.

By midafternoon, little did I know that my next doctor's appointment would set the agenda for my full recovery. When we entered the room, we were met by a beautiful young woman whose smile was transferrable. She called my name, reached out her hand to greet me and my sister, and asked us to please follow her.

After we reached the room assigned to us, we took a seat, and she proceeded to take my vitals. Once completed, she asked the doctor to come in. About three minutes went by, and the door opened the door. For some strange reason, the first thing that I noticed were his shoes. They were sharp. Shiny and indicated that he took pride in what he did.

I smiled when he said, "Well, you must be Brenda?" Looking up at this never-ending statue of a human being, I smiled and said, "Indeed I am." He then said, "Hello, my name is Dr. Frame, and I will be performing your surgery." Instantly, I felt reassured that I had been placed in good hands.

I was immediately put to a sense of peace. I looked beyond the person. I strained to hear God's voice in the moment through him. I watched his every move, how he talked to me. How he took the time to explain to me every precaution about the surgery. Even how he took pride in how he handled me. Little did anyone else in that room know, I was already thanking God that His gracious hand was resting upon me and causing my body to be healed, even before the surgery ever took place.

As we continued to talk, he asked me some specific questions about my health, and how did the discovery of the cancer ever come about? I told him that I had found it myself and that I had already scheduled my yearly mammogram appointment, which was coming up within a couple of weeks, and I had made preparation to have additional testing done as well.

Before the testing began, I asked the doctor if he would care to see my x-rays and additional notes that were given to me from the first doctor that I had seen, and he said, "Why, I would love too." Mind you, prior to him saying yes, no one else cared to.

After looking at the x-rays, he asked his nurse to please bring in the ultrasound equipment. He took one look at the x-rays and asked me to lie down on the table, and then went directly to where the problem was.

When the examination was over, I sat up on the table. We sat side by side, almost arm to arm and discussed the next step of the journey. He talked to me about my situation. He included me in the decision making, which I thought was interesting, because all too often, a patient is normally told what the doctor is going to do and is not ever to ask whether or not they have any input in the matter. He didn't make the final choices for me. He took the time to care and to show immense compassion and professionalism for my input as well. For that, I was grateful.

I asked, would I have to have a mastectomy? He looked me in the eye. "Absolutely not." He said, "Brenda, this is what I specialize in, and I can tell you that looking at your x-ray, by the time that I am finished, you will barely notice what the procedure was." To God be the glory that is rightfully due His name.

He said, "A little birdy told me that you requested to have your surgery while you are here this week, and if that is the case, we can plan to have it on Thursday morning, if that is okay with you?"

I agreed, and it was scheduled. He said, "Is there anything else I should know? Smiling and feeling totally relaxed, I asked, "Yes, if possible, after surgery, could you make sure that I could have breakfast in my room? I would like a ham, bacon, and cheese omelet, hash browns, and toast, please."

Honestly, I thought my sister was going to ultimately pass out right then and there. The very look on her face said, "Are you serious? That look alone was totally priceless!

The doctor said one more thing Brenda. "Can you tell me why you chose to attend our facility as opposed to having your surgery in Texas?"

For me, personally, after praying and fasting, I had no doubts or regrets that this was the supernatural way for me to have my surgery performed. There was total peace and absolute surrendering about the entire process. No regrets of any kind.

Within a couple of days, the date was set for my surgery on Thursday, May 8, 2014, at around 6:30 a.m. The chaplain came in and prayed with me and my sister prior to surgery, and I was prepped and then taken into surgery by one of the nurses.

The next thing that I knew, I was out of surgery and told that I had come through it like a champ, all praise and glory to my Lord and Savior. After returning to my room, I was able to take a nap and then sit up for a while. My sister took very good care of me. She was an incredible caregiver. The next morning, which was Friday May 9, 2014, I had a follow- up appointment with the nurse advocate to take a look at the scarring to make sure that everything was as it was supposed to be. At first I was very hesitant to look, but with the nurse advocate and my caregiver's support, I changed my mind and followed suit. To my surprise and relief, I was extremely thankful and very, very blessed to notice very minimal scarring at all.

Saturday morning, May 10, 2014, I was able to travel by plane and return home to continue healing. Upon arrival at home, I was surrounded by genuine love and an outpouring of support. I could not have asked for a better support and a genuine team. The gracious arm of God definitely went before me and caused all my enemies to be defeated.

Daily, my strength was being renewed like that of an eagle. Each day, I began to relinquish my faith, hope, and my peace into the hands of the Almighty God. I knew that without Him, I could do nor accomplish anything.

There were at times, during this process, that I literally felt as though my feet were never touching the ground. I could feel myself being carried along the way. At no time did I have a feeling of fear or being overwhelmed, even though this was new territory for me, I believed that God had, and still has, an incredible journey for me.

The next week, on a Tuesday morning around 10:00 a.m., my telephone rang, and it was my doctor who had performed the surgery calling me; and it just so happened that I actually answered the phone. His voice sounding ecstatic said, "Hello, Brenda. Is this Brenda?"

I said, "Yes, it is."

His reply was, "Hello, this is Dr. Frame, calling with your biopsy results. How are you feeling?"

Excited because of how confident he sounded on the phone, I said, "Great, what's going on?"

He said, "Well, we have your test results back from the biopsy, and they were great. There are no additional signs of cancer. We took up to five lymph nodes out, and each of them was what we had been hoping for. We are assured we got it all during surgery."

I screamed and thanked God to the highest. My only regret was that I did so directly in his good ear. He laughed and said that he understood. My big brother, who had been sitting at the table along with my sister and my husband, heard me screaming and asked, "What's wrong?" When I explained, he literally leaped up from the table and lifted his arms up in the air and said, "Thank you, Jesus," with tears of joy streaming down his face. He tried to apologize, but by then, everyone present was praising God for themselves.

With that great big beautiful smile, I watched his tears of joy flow down his face like liquid praise and worship all at the same time. I could instantly tell that my brother was genuinely rejoicing with me.

In that moment alone, I believed that the spiritual time clock of heaven paused and froze us in time. We realized that in that instance, truly the gracious arm of God had just rested upon us. We were quiet and intentionally worshipped God individually, in our own way. For the next hour or so, all each of us did was deliberately worship Him in our own likeness.

The dynamics of that hour literally changed my outlook on how I looked at this particular part of the journey for my life. I knew somewhere in my spiritual being that I was more than okay. I realized that I was more than a conqueror. I did not need the assurance from another human being. I didn't need or require the validation from man. I didn't have to be reassured that their opinion of me or my temporary setback needed confirmation because I knew that God had the final outcome of it all.

My doctor informed me that within the next three weeks or so, someone from the center would be contacting me about the treatment setup. I was told to relax and rest in my healing. I was already a step ahead of them in that regard. For the next several weeks, I continued to pray, "Sovereign God, go before me and make the crooked places straight. I trust you, Lord."

Night and day, this was my mantra. I chose not to look to the left or to the right. I valued no one else's final word but the Almighty God's. I realized that I was indeed in a battle for my natural well-being, and there was only one name that was above every name that could heal and rescue me, and that was the one name that I chose to rely on and rest in. So I dug my heels in and steadied the course. I thought I must see this through.

During this time, I was extremely guarded in who I spoke with, shared my heart with, and even my emotions with. One important footnote that I had to remember was that while going through the valley of what is considered the "Shadow of Death," the only person really necessary in that moment is the "tour guide," who has travelled that route the most. Not only does He know the safest way to bring one out, but He is the One who has already orchestrated the route over 2,000 years ago, on my behalf, and said, "Brenda, don't worry, all is well."

Even when the little pains and aches came, I laid hands on my body and whispered, "Lord, even in this I trust you. I remember the spoken promises that were spoken over my life years ago and I gently reminded my Redeemer, Lord you said according to Psalms 91:1–16:

> *With long life will I satisfy him, and shew him my salvation. He that dwelleth in the secret place of the most High shall abide under the shadow of the Almighty. I will say of the LORD, He is my refuge and my fortress: my God; in him will I trust. Surely he shall deliver thee from the snare of the fowler, and from the noisome pestilence.*
>
> *He shall cover thee with his feathers, and under his wings shalt thou trust: his truth shall be thy shield and buckler. Thou*

shalt not be afraid for the terror by night; nor for the arrow that flieth by day; Nor for the pestilence that walketh in darkness; nor for the destruction that wasteth at noonday.

A thousand shall fall at thy side, and ten thousand at thy right hand; but it shall not come nigh thee. Only with thine eyes shalt thou behold and see the reward of the wicked. Because thou hast made the LORD, which is my refuge, even the most High, thy habitation; There shall no evil befall thee, neither shall any plague come nigh thy dwelling.

For he shall give his angels charge over thee, to keep thee in all thy ways. They shall bear thee up in their hands, lest thou dash thy foot against a stone. Thou shalt tread upon the lion and adder: the young lion and the dragon shalt thou trample under feet.

Because he hath set his love upon me, therefore will I deliver him: I will set him on high, because he hath known my name. He shall call upon me, and I will answer him: I will be with him in trouble; I will deliver him, and honour him.

I decided that the gracious arm of God would indeed rest upon me even in my "now" moment, which appeared to be my darkest times. Surely, He alone would come through for me and my household because we rest in Him.

During the third week, I received a call from the Cancer Treatment Centers about my treatment. The nurse advocate said, "Brenda, we are calling about the next leg of your journey as it relates to your treatment. Looking at your test results, we find that instead of six weeks of treatment at twice a day, we find that you will only need three weeks and once a day, at fifteen minutes at a time. There will be no need for chemotherapy at this time."

For those of you who are not ashamed of the gospel, I would hope that you would join in with me and echo the sentiments when I say, "Won't He do it!" Not only did I thank Him, but I did so before I ever made the trip back. "Sovereign God, thank you for healing my body and turning things around for me in my health from my head to my toes one more time."

My prayer in that moment was, "Daddy, turn it around for your daughter, one more time." And then I rested in His expressed assurance. As the time drew closer for me to return to the center for treatment, I began to share the news with my family, and they were once again gearing up for that emotional ride with me.

Thinking that I had made myself clear that they would not be taking this journey, in terms of "going with me" this time, I prepared myself, as best I could, to travel naturally speaking, alone. I was supposed to leave Fort Worth on Friday evening to arrive on late Friday afternoon and begin my treatments on Monday morning.

Little did I know God had another plan—the closer we got to Friday, the more my family began to say, "Bren, we think that you should take this leg of your journey with your family." We know that you can do this alone, but it would be better if you took us along with you as moral support. We love you and don't want to see you go through this by yourself."

Honestly, that day was one of the proudest days of my journey because they were willing to put physical action to their faith and join in the journey with me. I was smiling inside. I didn't know exactly how God was going to make the crooked ways plain in terms of financially; but I knew if He brought me to it, He would bring me through it, so I rested in Him.

The interesting thing about my journey is that I know for myself that no matter what happens in my life, how many falls and slipups I may have to endure, disappointments that will arise in my life, doors that will be closed to me, or folks who will walk out of my life, and even when the tears from hardship may roll down my cheeks, God still have a "one more time for His baby girl."

On Wednesday evening, I thought that I was alone, so I eased outside and began watering the front lawn, right before the sun went down, thinking that everyone else in the house was preoccupied and wouldn't notice. As I am standing there watering the grass, I began to reminisce about the sheer goodness of Jehovah in my life.

I remembered all the times He has lifted me, carried me, stayed His hands over my life. How He had favored me with His grace and mercies. How He has sheltered me and gone before me to make sure that my enemies wouldn't defeat me.

I told Him how grateful I was. How honored I was just to be one of the daughters of the Most High God. That I recognized that it was only because He lives that I could remotely face my tomorrows, and that my life was worth the living just because He lived in me. The more I acknowledged His presence, the more He made His face to shine on me. I felt renewed in an instant. I felt blessed beyond measure. Somehow, I knew that all was well.

A few minutes later, I felt the presence of someone beside or near me. Without turning around, I heard this male voice say, "Faye, I know that you are strong and that you probably can handle going it alone; however, I have come to tell you that we have talked about your trip to Tulsa and decided that we are going with you, no questions asked. I am going to drive you, and we are going with you for moral support." I felt the tears welling up, so I tried to turn and walk away, as if I were looking for something in the grass. The more I moved away from him, the more he pursued me.

Once again, he said, "Baby, this is the time for family to stick together. I didn't know exactly what I was facing when I came to Texas, or for how long I would be staying, but now that I am here and I see, I know what I have to do. We are going with you, and that's it."

My brother didn't know, but God knew what I needed, and He sent those words of encouragement and support in the form of my big brother Eddie and my sister Dorothy. During those several months, they were my husband's and my lifeline. They worked in harmony. They were our moral support team; they gave of their time, substance, deed, and generosity.

They left no earthly stone unturned. Day and night, they served with servant's hearts, and they did it with a cheerful heart. Make no mistake, when true servants serve, you can actually see a Godly reflection in their service.

There are no hidden agendas with true servants. They don't need the applause of mankind. They don't feel the need to broadcast their services or keep a litany of notes of all they did for the validation of man. They serve out of what they have. They understand that God will reward them for what they have done, and they are happy to oblige. In the weeks and months while I was in treatment, I watched my big brother, whom I love dearly, serve my husband and I, unto God. He did so with every fiber of his being, asking for nothing in return.

There was absolutely nothing asked of him that he didn't willfully do with a cheerful heart. It wasn't that he necessarily understood everything that was asked of him at the outset, but it was his willingness to do so, sometimes without question.

I am assured that God Almighty honored his efforts. My brother served my husband like he was his brother in blood. He withheld no good thing from him. I watched quietly as the two became close and ministered to each other. God indeed knows how to repair what is broken in each of us. During that time, I was reminded of the particular scripture in the book of Matthews 25:39–40, which says,

When did we see You sick, or in prison, and come to You?' "The King will answer and say to them, 'Truly I say to you, to the extent that you did it to one of these brothers of Mine, even the least of them, you did it to Me.

You see, one thing that I know for sure is that the world is very quick to cast down, throw away those that they deem are not popular, successful, unworthy, washed up, missed it in life, and left for dead. But God, the Maker, Lord, Creator, and Ruler over the entire universe knows each of His sheep, and He is the one that has the final ruling and say.

Thank you, Jesus. It is well. It is, indeed, well. I watched my brother grow within that first month by mere leaps and spiritual bounds. Daily, his demeanor changed. His attitude grew deeper, with every opportunity to see the hand of God at work in my life, my husband's life, our sister's life, including his life. He realized probably now, more than ever, what it means to be spiritually transformed by God.

I am so grateful that the Word of God declares that it is not by our might or our power, but by His Word says, the Lord of Hosts. It was wonderful to see. From time to time, the enemy would try to intercept his joy and steal his peace. But he dug his heels in and held his ground. Little by little, I don't know if he recognized that he was changing and being transformed for the greater or not, but in actuality, he was.

My sister Dorothy was a jewel. To know her is to have the best of both worlds. Dorothy is indeed a sister-sister. She will go through both the thick and thin with you. The highs and the lows. She can truly rejoice with those who are rejoicing and cry with those who are travailing. She is genuine in spirit. She is one of the most humble human beings that I know. I call myself blessed to have in her a sisterhood in the natural, and a sister-in-Christ, working in the kingdom-of-God relationship with her.

The day of my first radiation treatment, I spent a lot of time alone in private prayer with my Heavenly Daddy. I shared with Him my innermost thoughts and fears. He counseled me, kept me, and assured me that all was indeed well. Recognizing that once these foreign chemicals entered my body there would be no turning back.

Ironically, the Spirit of the Living God reminded me that before the chemicals were ever mentioned, the blood of Jesus had already permeated my entire body because of His death, burial, and resurrection. What a Mighty God we serve!

I was able to walk 3.5 miles in the early mornings, and sometimes in the afternoon before treatments, if it wasn't too hot. I was often cheered on by my family, nurses, doctors, and other patients. Throughout my treatment, I was able to counsel, pray with others, attend various church services, and lead a normal life with very minimal side effects. To Him be all the glory!

Each day we watched as the Lord strategically provided and kept His gracious arms around us. To that end, we never experienced, even the least kind of lack in any area of our lives. For the first time in a year and a half, I watched my husband being able to travel and sleep in another bed other than a hospital bed. I watched him get out of the room and have daily exercise and consistent showers with the assistance of my brother by his side.

Knowing that I had the earthly support through those who genuinely loved me whether it was through the personal touch of siblings being able to be there with me physically, through personal phone calls, cards, monetary giving, food, visits after we were back home or just meaningful well wishes on a consistent basis, it was all greatly appreciated.

Although I don't always get to spend time with my nephews and nieces, when we do get together, it is like we have never quite been apart. In fact, for some of them, it is difficult to think of them as nieces and nephews because we grew up together and walked a major part of our livelihoods as one and the same. For me personally, they are more like brothers and sisters. I thank God that I can call upon them and know that they will be right there, as they have been on so many occasions. Leon, Darreyl, Rubye, Bettye, Lisa, Sherrye, and Chandra and to a very special niece who has transitioned home to live forever with the Lord, Sharon, I love and value you all with my heart. I am thankful they are a part of my journey in some aspect as well.

During the Fourth of July holiday weekend, another one of my sisters, Vera and my nephew, Jeffery, came up to visit from Memphis.

Just seeing them was a true blessing. We laughed a lot and treasured our time together. In a whole lot of ways, our time together was refreshing and enjoyable. We ate a lot, listened to oldies but goodies, and took several trips back down memory lane!

My big sister loved on me, and I enjoyed every bit of it. In fact, I basked in it all. The fact that God would give me this time with her made the visit even the more special. On Sunday morning, the five of us went to church and out to lunch afterward.

We chose to celebrate life and be very grateful of what God had done in the lives of all of us, rather than complain and mumble and grumble about the whys and how comes. Their leaving on Tuesday made for a bittersweet moment, but it was still very rewarding to cherish the time that we had spent together.

One of the specific things that my oncologist shared with me about returning back to work was that I needed to pace myself and not allow myself to become overwhelmed or stressed out about things. Understanding that my body had experienced a very traumatic journey and it needed all the time in the world to heal before diving back into life full speed ahead.

Statistics show that one of major contributors to cancer is worry, stress, and thinking negatively. These are all the things I encounter on a daily basis as do others in our society. In fact, one of the major issues, from my doctor's perspective, was that I was under consistent stressful situations for a long period of time, and this in some ways contributed to my body not being able to handle the impact of it all.

Even as I type today and recall just some of the things God allowed me to tunnel through are simply amazing in itself. He kept me in the midst of them all. Including working two jobs for four years—getting up at 3:00 a.m. after going to bed sometimes at 1:00 a.m.

I lived at the hospital and rehabilitation center while my husband was hospitalized, taking care of the affairs of daily living and expenses, trying to find reputable help, which did not always work out to our favor. I am honored that in the midst of it all, the Lord God taught me how to endure hardships as a good solider, knowing that what was designed to kill me, and perhaps cause harm to me and my family, would only serve as a weapon that God would use to turn it all around in our favor.

God used what was meant to weaken me and to perhaps render me helpless and hopeless as fuel to reignite and to accelerate my faith to several new levels. In fact, He proved through my trials that I was not just a conqueror, I was more than a conqueror. Thank you, Jesus. Amen!

Returning to work was exciting and rewarding. For me, personally, it meant naturally speaking that God had enabled me to be able to work and take care of myself and my family. Thank God for family members and true friends who were there for us as well during those days of challenges. They prayed, stayed, gave, and showed up when it mattered the most. But what I was most proud of was that what these individuals did for me and my families wasn't placed on YouTube, Twitter, Facebook, or phone-a-friend club and tell everyone you know what you have done.

I consider myself to be a very private person, and I am under the belief that what an individual makes happen for someone else doesn't need to be exposed by the true giver. Give it time, and the receiver will share, if necessary.

My coworkers were loving as well; they were very supportive and giving. They were generous with their contributions and encouraging words. A very, very sincere thank-you goes out to Ms. Robin. She was so instrumental in the beginning of it all. I will always be very appreciative of her guidance and support of me.

I could not have asked for or imagined a more com-passionate, loving, caring, and dedicated boss, manager, supervisor, and friend than the one God blessed me with. This woman possesses strength, integrity, graciousness, and resolve like no other. She was there for me and my husband from day one. She came to the hospital. She was there by my side when emergency calls came through for me to respond.

She never looked the other way. She never judged me or ridiculed me. Instead, I found her to be a constant; she was by my side, giving me and my family love and support beyond measure. It is my personal prayer for her and her family that our God will pour back into her life a hundred-fold what she has given to me and mine. In my thoughts and prayers, she is a jewel to be treasured for the remainder of my days.

There were those who appeared very shocked, to say the least, that I had returned to work—and even more shocked that I still had my very own hair. Life can be really funny sometimes. I didn't mind that they thought that way, quite frankly. The good laughter came right on cue, little did they know.

As the days moved forward, God kept going before me, making all of my crooked paths plain. He favored me and my family with His goodness, mercy, and unlimited and unmerited favor. He comforted me. Held me and ordered my steps strategically. Daily, He provided us with every necessary amenity that my family and I needed. We suffered absolutely no lack. Even those things that the enemy stole from us, God was faithful to replace in His own way.

What I learned in those moments was to refuse to allow the enemy to steal, borrow, lease, rent, or even negotiate my joy. It wasn't for sale or disturbance. For everything the enemy stole, I was instinctively informed by the Holy Spirit to relinquish. And I literally watched God restore anew in me and my disposition about it all. That, my dear, was priceless! At some point, I began asking God for the purpose of it all. I knew beyond a shadow of a doubt that something bigger was being developed in me and through my personal journey of it all.

This may sound crazy to a lot of people, but instead of worrying or being angry about my journey, I learned to relax, release, and to enjoy it all. I really wanted to genuinely learn from my personal experience. I spent my days and night talking to God and listening a lot for His wisdom and direction.

He never failed me. Not one time was I disappointed in it all. I learned that the doors that were opened for me were the doors that I was to enter. The doors that were closed or appeared to be stuck were not mine to enter at the time, or perhaps never. Therefore, I didn't allow myself to become bombarded or frustrated with the whys or why nots. I decided to move forward and trust God for direction.

I cannot tell you how rewarding and refreshing it is to truly "cast all of your cares upon the Lord" and leave them there. For He alone truly cares for us. Not only did I discover personally that I have an infinite hope in the Everlasting Father and my intimate relationship with Him, I learned that I can rely and depend upon Him always.

I don't have to worry or fret that He will ever run out of grace, unlimited mercies, unmerited favor, and abundance of joy, peace, longsuffering, love, guidance, or any other resources that I will have need of. In Him alone I truly found refuge. A safe haven in which I can incline my voice to, and know that He will hear my prayers and answer assuredly. I grasp the fact that it is in Him that I live, move, and have my being.

My personal love life with God has sailed to newer heights and deeper depths. I rest my salvation and eternal life solely in His hands. I depend on no other like I do the Lord. He is with me all the time. I accept the fact that whatever comes my way and actually gets to me has passed through the divine hands of God, and therefore has been ordered by Him; and if he allows it to pass through, undoubtedly, He has a planned blessing for me on the other side of it.

Today, I am so very thankful that I know God in an intimate way for myself. Because as I live and breathe today, I have met people from all walks of life, backgrounds, and religious beliefs that have tried to sway me in one direction or the other, as it relates to their thoughts, understanding, belief system, or just their personal opinions about how I should look at my life since being diagnosed with cancer.

There is absolutely no doubt in my mind, heart, and soul that I am completely healed from the crown of my head to the soles of my feet. That I am healed and that God alone has done a marvelous thing in my body and in my health. His Word alone has secured me in that fact.

I trust Him completely without fail. Because of his past track record of being there every single time I needed Him, and even when I didn't know that I needed Him, is all the proof that I need. The days of trying to convince others or touching and agreeing with others and trying to get them to understand and/or accept that God is indeed a healer is far gone from my determination.

Admittedly, I am taken aback often when I encounter those of the faith that are most challenging in their overall belief as it relates to healing. Whenever I mentioned to them about what God has done for me as it relates to healing my body, it's interesting that while some are willing to hear about the prognosis, they are sometimes reluctant to accept the fact that Almighty God still can heal even in today's time.

For instance, there is a certain person that I have known for more than twenty years, and even though I believe she is a Christian (she can be found most days quoting scriptures, she has the most up-to-date gadgets, bibles and iPads, and is well versed in the Word of God); however, for her, just listening to me declare my healing and speaking about the word of exhortation, complete healing or being healed by God in today's time, is mind-boggling for her.

She will ask me over and over again, "So, how is everything? What's going on with you and your cancer?" And my response is always the same, "I am delivered. Healed, whole, and resting in the Almighty God. Now, when you see the cancer, perhaps, if you are still interested, you can ask it, since it is no longer a part of my life."

To someone reading this part of my book may deem me to be a

little arrogant or rude, I say, honestly, what I know for sure is that in order to walk in the true realm of what I believe that God has done for me, I must make up my mind once and for all whose report I truly am willing to believe with full understanding that the world has its understanding and concept, but God has the truth as it relates to me and the purpose of my being on earth.

And since His truth is based upon His Word, and His Word is Him, and every promise that He has made to me through His Word is mine, and if I will take hold to it and stand on it, I can have what it said to its fullness.

In this personal journey of mine, I refuse to send or give one second of my energy, talent, mind, power, or empowerment to the enemy. In fact, nowadays, I tell him if you want to talk with me, please look under my shoe where I have left you a message because you are under my feet in the name of Jesus. I agree totally with Proverbs 23:7. "As a man thinks in his heart, so is he…"

So, if I believe within my heart and choose to execute my faith as it relates to my complete healing in the Lord that I am healed, whole, delivered, resisting all sickness and diseases through faith and wisdom, doing what the Word of God tells me, I shall have what I say. Of course, the final word is up to God in any situation, trial, testing, or circumstance; however, how I choose to handle my personal storm is what matters most in the moment.

I realize that even when my mind is made up the enemy will still try with all his might to change, alter, and intercept the will and plan and purpose for my life; however, if I will just remain in the will of God, I will see that God still has me in the palm of His hands.

It is amazing just how powerful and influential the mind really is. I understand that what I tend to focus on the most is actually, in my opinion, what truly rules the very core of me in that "moment." For instance, if I harbor unforgiveness in my heart about someone and allow my entire being to be dragged into my emotions as I meditate upon that entire situation or person, I notice how my body tends to stiffen, and I become agitated, irritated, upset, overwhelmed, and even feeling downtrodden to the point of almost being immobilized over that very situation.

However, the moment I realize that unforgiveness as being an unresolved issue in my heart, instead of allowing it to further affect my entire day and momentarily my mood and eventually my emotions, I know that I must go to the Lord and ask for help in resolving and correcting the issue. I know that without making this step, I will be left with a misguided focus, the inability to function as I should, and more importantly, I know that God will not be blessed with my actions, and that's what matters to me the most. However, when I repent and align my thoughts with the word and will of God, those old, tired, and stressful moments dissipate quickly.

I am learning more and more through my faith and God's truth that the most important concept about how I see myself and others is only vital and necessary when it is done through the lens of Christ. Trying to truly judge a book by any other method, unless I have read the book, is a complete and utter waste of time and unnecessary spent energy, to say the least.

How one sees themselves through blurred vision at best will always be misdiagnosed because the lens in which our natural eyesight is looking through and is dependent upon to provide us accurate information is already outdated from the beginning because we do not fully have all the details or knowledge about our days ahead. At best, we only know to some extent what is directly in front of us now. We must remember that as human beings, we are incapable of such accurate knowledge in and of ourselves. Only God knows the plan that he has established in the heavens and the earth for us.

Trusting God and allowing our raw faith to be executed daily will teach us a renewed, refreshed, and revitalizing witness of just who God really is in our daily lives. We must not allow our faith to become standard, staggered, or stale. We must keep on trusting God even when the odds seem to be literally stacking against us rather than downsizing.

We've got to learn to cry out to God from a place that was seemingly off limits before or unreserved and considered private and known just to us. We must learn how to become unleashed and unraveled, cutting away all strings, binding things that would stop us from entering into the presence of the most High God. We must learn that we must not enter but learn how to respect the place and the presence to which we have entered.

To me, raw faith is an expectation of something greater than what I can independently provide for myself. Raw faith is relying upon, leaning on, solely dependent upon the greater source to provide for me, lead me, to guide and mentor me through life's daily pathway. It's reliance upon the greater to maneuver me through this maze called life because I realize that in and of myself, I cannot make anything happen in my own might.

It's more than just coming to God with my semi-opened-mind level of intelligence. With my fingers crossed and a limited belief, faith, and hope that God could do it; however, even while praying I am really not sure if He will do for me in my dire time of need.

I know now more than ever that even when my knees are seemingly buckling beneath the load that I have been equipped to carry, when the testing of that personal trial seems to be lingering longer than I personally anticipated or desired, when it seems to be testing the very fiber of my spiritual being or going beyond the level of my personal strength, it is when those difficult, blind- siding issues and circumstances come out of nowhere that can often knock me to my knees—even then I can still remind God of his promises.

I must be like Abraham when he said in Romans 4:19 that he "consider(ed) not the report." We too must not consider our negative financial checking/savings account. Consider not a negative health report. Consider not whether our God has a spouse waiting for us or not. Consider not our unemployment situation. Consider not a bad or intense addiction. And consider not a trial that doesn't seem to be turning around. We must always remember that in God, there is no failure!

In tough times, we must remind ourselves in the Lord according to the following scriptures: 1 Corinthians 2:9, Ephesians 3:20–21, and Philippians 4:19.

> *But as it is written, Eye hath not seen, nor ear heard, neither have entered into the heart of man, the things which God hath prepared for them that love him. (1 Cor. 2:9)*
>
> *Now to Him who is able to do exceedingly abundantly above all that we ask or think, according to the power that works in us, to Him be glory in the church by Christ Jesus to all generations, forever and ever. Amen. Eph. 3:20–21)*
>
> *And this same God who takes care of me will supply all your needs from his glorious riches, which have been given to us in Christ Jesus. (Phil. 4:19)*

As opposed to going around daily with a scornful look on our faces, being oppressed and depressed over our woes and temporary circumstances, we've got to remember that we've got to continue looking up as scripture further reminds us to

> *Lift up your heads, O gates, And lift them up, O ancient doors, That the King of glory may come in! Who is this King of glory? The LORD of hosts, He is the King of glory. Selah. (Ps. 24:9, NLT)*

Overall, I never wanted or required personal glory or glorification, but I did want His anointing to reign over and into my life. Many days I would cry literally and figuratively for a closer walk with God. I wanted my steps to be ordered and ordained by Him. Little did I know and fully understand the cost that came along with that request. What I did know for sure was that God alone was able to carry me through.

By now, I was learning that faith for me was not about quoting scriptures and walking around things seven times. It was so far removed from naming and claiming things for the mere sake of it and expecting the unknown to suddenly appear through osmosis, but rather, faith required diligence, wisdom, deliberate, and intentional muscle action. Faith is a muscle that must be regularly exercised and put to use. It must be challenged, stretched, and tried.

~ The Takeaway: What I Know Now for Sure ~

For as he thinketh in his heart, so is he:
Eat and drink, saith he to thee; but
his heart is not with thee.
—Proverbs 23:7 (KJV)

    In conclusion of this book, my greatest desire is that my readers will walk away knowing that raw faith to me, is the attitude and the mindset that one takes in the face of life that will either cause me to believe the unaltered Word of God for myself, or allow my personal daily circumstances to dictate to me as to how I should respond to or act in the face of adversity.

    God's name is above all other names. He does not have to get the buy-in of others' opinions, thoughts, or reasoning before He will respond to my pleas and my needs. He is omnipotent and omnipresent. He is Lord overall and in all.

    Finally, taking away from this book that our God is indeed an awesome God, and indeed, He does reign forevermore. Believe that with God, all things are possible. He can make happen in our personal lives what would take us a lifetime to accomplish without faith. God is, and will always be, continuously for His people. He does not have any respecter of persons. He covers the just, as well as the unjust; and it is His will to bless and keep all that was created by Him.

My hope is that if you are not seeking God with your whole heart at the time of reading this book, by the end of the chapters, you will make Him a priority in your life. Learn how to place nothing and no one else above Him. Allow Him alone to order your steps and your day. Refuse to go about the earth and its business without His guidance. Seek after Him with your whole heart, mind, and soul. Cry out to Him for direction, insight, and wisdom; and I can assure you, He will hear and meet you exactly where you are.

Let me challenge you that just in case He may not come the way and the moment that you think that He should, don't give up and don't turn away from Him thinking that He may not care or doesn't hear you, because in both cases, He does. In some instances, He may desire to see how much you need Him; and other times, you are just moments away from your breakthrough.

I have learned in both instances to be determined, bold, and confident that our God is a good God and that He reigns over absolutely everything. He is sovereign, and He alone is just. He is capable of hearing us before we even call Him; and He alone is the necessary answer to each and every finite problem that we have. He alone is consistent. He is able, and He is more than enough. He is unlimited in all manners of power. No one can stay His hand or change His mind toward us. He not only cares about us, but He loves us beyond measure as well.

I found out personally that I could trust Him for every single need to be met, and then some. That I could also rest in Him explicitly without a shadow of a doubt. There is something Great, Specific, and Assured about the name of Jesus. There is absolute soundness, peace, and fortitude in his Name. Not only is it a name that is above each and every other name, but it echoes truth that He alone reigns over everything.

It does not matter what phase of life we find ourselves in. No condition, problem, circumstance, or situation is too overwhelming that He cannot solve and resolve. He is the can-do and will-do it. God!

I am utterly convinced that with God all things are possible, and no matter when we call upon Him for help, guidance, peace, hope, love, and joy, He promises to hear our prayers and come to our rescue, and to become a very present help in the midst of our troubles.

> *I will answer them before they even call to me. While they are still talking about their needs, I will go ahead and answer their prayers! (Isa. 65:24, NLT)*

Not only was He God back then to those that needed Him, He is the true and living God in my right-now. He sits upon His throne and watches carefully over His word to its fulfillment according to Jeremiah 1:12. (NIV) "The LORD said to me, 'You have seen correctly, for I am watching to see that my word is fulfilled.'"

Accordingly, Isaiah 55:10–11 (ESV) makes it plain when it says,

> *For as the rain and the snow come down from heaven, And do not return there but water the earth Making it bring forth and sprout,*
>
> *Giving seed to the sower and bread to the eater; So shall my word be that goes out from my mouth; It shall not return to me empty,*
>
> *But it shall accomplish that which I purpose And shall succeed in the thing for which I sent it.*

Whatever God says, He alone will carry it out to its fruition and will watch over it to see that it will not be delayed, compromised, reduced, or forgotten. Praise you, Jesus.

> *Go confidently into the direction of your dreams.*
> *Live the life you've imagined.*
> —Henry David Thoreau

About the Author

Brenda has served as a worship leader, intercessory prayer leader, Sunday school Superintendent, counselor as well as hosted family life conferences for women retreats, mother and daughter brunches and single events.

Uniquely, Brenda weaves her life story, and her powerful teaching to create a message of encouragement, hope and motivation. A message that challenges everyone to keep their eyes focused on the real prize and that is none other than Jesus Christ who is LORD over everything.

Brenda holds a Bachelor Degree in Human Resources from the University of Phoenix, Arizona. She attended the Southwestern Baptist Theological Seminary where she enrolled in Leadership for Women in Fort Worth, Texas. Brenda has served as the Founder of her own ministry called Innovative Ministries, Inc. for over 15 years. She is also a member of National Association for Women Professionals (NAFW).

She has received numerous certificates and awards for her various rolls in Christian Leadership as well. Brenda is currently awaiting an opportunity to serve on the board of Directors for Puttin on the Pink for the interval of 2017-2018.

Brenda is happily married to the absolute love of her life Audie for 31 years and enjoys resting in the perfect will, purpose and plan of God for their lives. Currently, Brenda and Audie reside in the great city of Fort Worth, Texas.

www.ingramcontent.com/pod-product-compliance
Lightning Source LLC
LaVergne TN
LVHW051602070426
835507LV00021B/2721